Editor
Brent L. Fox, M. Ed.

Editor in Chief
Karen J. Goldfluss, M.S. Ed.

Creative Director
Sarah M. Fournier

Cover Artist
Sarah Kim

Illustrator
Kelly McMahon

Art Coordinator
Renée Mc Elwee

Imaging
Amanda R. Harter

Publisher
Mary D. Smith, M.S. Ed.

Author
Ruth Foster, M. Ed.

For correlations to the Common Core State Standards, visit *http://www.teachercreated.com/standards/*.

Teacher Created Resources
12621 Western Avenue
Garden Grove, CA 92841
www.teachercreated.com
ISBN: 978-1-4206-8124-6

Made in U.S.A.

Table of Contents

Table of Contents *(cont.)*

Introduction

Reading should be something that students look forward to. However, sometimes students must find fun and accessible literature *before* they can realize how enjoyable reading can be! The passages in this book contain high-interest topics that will immediately hook even the most stubborn of readers. Fun themes, surprise twists, and grade-appropriate content will motivate and excite young readers. Additionally, the passages in this book were designed to be accessible to students of varying reading abilities. Basic sight words are introduced and then reinforced with repetition and practice. As new words are introduced, they are repeated and written into the story in ways that allow a student to use context clues to decipher their meanings.

Each unit begins with five reading passages. The first several passages are short and include four multiple-choice questions. The remaining passages are a bit longer and have five multiple-choice questions. The passages in each unit are a mixture of fact and fiction. The last page of the unit calls for a written response to a prompt that incorporates the theme of the unit.

The passages in each unit are all linked by a loose theme. As the students continue to read more of the unit, they will begin to discover the common thread that weaves together each collection of stories. This approach broadens a student's comprehension and understanding of the subject matter. It allows students to practice new words in various stories and in different genres. It also shows students how separate passages can be linked with other passages and used collectively to expand one's horizons and views. This approach ultimately allows students to become familiar with the flexibility of word use, different viewpoints, and how we can learn from both fiction and nonfiction texts.

All of the texts and activities in the *Let's Get This Day Started* series have been aligned to the Common Core State Standards (CCSS). Visit *http://www.teachercreated.com/standards/* for all standards correlations.

Using the Book

Teachers should not feel restricted by a daily warm-up activity. Sometimes, schedules change. A morning assembly, a make-up lesson, or just an extra-busy day can easily throw off the classroom schedule for days. A teacher never knows what his or her week is going to look like. *Let's Get This Day Started* does not need to be completed every day or even every other day. Teachers can take their time and arrange the activities to fit their own schedules. The book is written so the teacher can stop wherever and whenever he or she wants. A teacher may choose to do a unit a week (one passage a day), or at other times, spread a unit out over a few weeks. There is no right or wrong way.

At the beginning of the year, a teacher may choose to have the class read the passages together as a group before asking them to read each passage again on their own. A teacher may also choose to have students reread passages several weeks later to practice fluidity or so that the students can see how "easy" the passages have become.

The multiple-choice questions in *Let's Get This Day Started* assess all levels of comprehension—from recall to critical thinking. The questions are based on fundamental reading skills found in scope-and-sequence charts across the nation. Examples of just some of the question styles used in this series include:

- recalling information
- sequencing in chronological order
- using prior knowledge
- identifying synonyms and antonyms
- visualizing
- knowing and using grade-level vocabulary
- recognizing the main idea
- using context clues to understand new words
- identifying supporting details
- making inferences
- understanding cause and effect
- drawing conclusions

All question stems and answers are written so that they are a continuation of reading practice and critical thinking. If an answer choice includes an unfamiliar word, the correct answer can still be found by the process of elimination. Remind students to read every answer choice! If the answer doesn't jump out at them, they can get it right by crossing out the wrong answers first.

The written response (Write On!) pages require students to look back at the passages they have read in each unit for facts, ideas, or vocabulary. Students are encouraged to respond creatively to a variety of fun writing prompts and then support their answers by referring back to examples from several of the reading passages.

Use the Tracking Sheet on page 108 to keep track of which passages you have given to your students, or distribute copies of the sheet for students to monitor their own progress.

Name: Jayla florence

Snorkeling

You want to put your face into the water and look at fish. You wear a mask to help you see. You use a snorkel to help you breathe. One end of the snorkel goes into your mouth, while the other end sticks up out of the water. You use the snorkel to breathe while your face stays in the water.

Elephants also like to play in the water. Elephants may be big, but they are good swimmers. They can swim for hours and go long distances. Their heads, legs, and backs can be completely underwater. How do the elephants breathe when they are under the water? How do they breathe while swimming so far?

Elephants have very long noses called *trunks*. Elephants stick their trunks out of the water! Elephants use their trunks as snorkels!

1. If someone goes a long distance, they
   - **a.** go swimming.
   - **b.** are huge.
   - **c.** go far.
   - **d.** are underwater.

2. One reason an elephant may go completely underwater is
   - **a.** to stay cool.
   - **b.** to look for a mask.
   - **c.** to get warm in the sun.
   - **d.** to keep its legs dry.

3. This story is mainly about
   - **a.** elephants.
   - **b.** how far elephants can swim.
   - **c.** how you can see fish.
   - **d.** how elephants use their trunks like snorkels.

4. A *synonym* is a word that means the same thing as another word. What word is a synonym for *huge*?

   a. long **b.** big **c.** end **d.** mask

Name: ____________________

The Periscope

Sam said, "There is a submarine in the lake. I can see its periscope."

Sam's sister Hope asked, "What is a periscope?"

Sam said, "It's a tube. It has mirrors in it. A submarine can be completely underwater. It can stay hidden. If people in the submarine want to look around, they can use the submarine's periscope. The periscope can be raised up. It can be used to look all around."

Sam took Hope to see the submarine. "There!" Hope shouted. "I see the periscope! It is getting closer! It is getting very near! Sam, it is too close! Sam, it's getting out of the water! Sam, something is very wrong!"

Sam couldn't answer. He could only stare in wonder. They hadn't been looking at a periscope! They had been looking at elephant's trunk!

1. When might a submarine use a periscope?
   - **a.** when it is completely out of the water
   - **b.** when it wants to make people think it is an elephant
   - **c.** when it wants to look around while staying hidden
   - **d.** when it is time to eat dinner

2. Sam stared in wonder because
   - **a.** he was very scared.
   - **b.** he was very happy.
   - **c.** he was very afraid.
   - **d.** he was very surprised.

3. What happened **second** in the story? Read all the answers.
   - **a.** Sam tells Hope what a periscope is.
   - **b.** Sam takes Hope to see the submarine.
   - **c.** Sam sees an elephant.
   - **d.** Sam says that there is a submarine in the lake.

4. Most likely, what happens next in the story?
   - **a.** Hope makes a periscope.
   - **b.** Sam goes for a ride in a submarine.
   - **c.** Hope goes swimming.
   - **d.** Sam calls the zoo.

Name: ______________________________

A Fable About Wishing

A fable is a kind of story. It is a story with a moral. A moral is like a little lesson.

There once was a boy who made a wish. He wished to be as strong as an elephant. When the boy made his wish, something happened. His nose began to change. It got longer and longer. It changed into a trunk!

"This isn't what I wished for!" the boy said angrily.

A voice responded, "You only have 639 muscles in your whole body. Do you know how many muscles an elephant has in its trunk? An elephant's trunk has over 40,000 muscles!"

The voice continued. "An elephant trunk is very strong. What if you weighed 700 pounds? An elephant could pick you up with its trunk! You got a trunk so you could be as strong as an elephant. You got what you wished for."

Moral: Be careful what you wish for.

1. How is a fable different from a fairy tale?

- **a.** A fable has lots of rhyming words.
- **b.** Every part of a fable is true.
- **c.** Fairy tales are like little lessons.
- **d.** A fable has a moral.

2. Why is an elephant's trunk so strong?

- **a.** It has over 400 muscles.
- **b.** It has over 4,000 muscles.
- **c.** It has over 40,000 muscles.
- **d.** It has over 400,000 muscles.

3. What might be another moral for this story?

- **a.** Always say the first thing that you think of.
- **b.** Think before you speak.
- **c.** Everyone knows what you mean.
- **d.** Don't worry about what you say.

4. In the story, you do not find out

- **a.** what the boy wished for.
- **b.** who gave the boy his wish.
- **c.** why the boy got an elephant's trunk.
- **d.** how the boy felt when he got his wish.

Name: ______________________________

Something Scary

Long ago, people told stories. Some of the stories were scary. Some of the stories were about the cyclops. Why was the cyclops so scary? Why was it so terrifying? The cyclops was a huge giant. It had only one eye. The eye was big! It was in the center of the giant's forehead.

How did these scary stories begin? Long ago, someone found a skull. The skull was very big. It had a big hole in the middle. The person had never seen such a skull before. The person thought, "The skull is big. It must be a giant's skull! The giant has one big eye. That is why there is a hole in the middle."

The truth is that there is no cyclops. Most likely, the person found an elephant's skull. The person had never seen an elephant's skull before. The skull was huge, just like an elephant's head. The hole in the middle was not for an eye. It was the opening for the elephant's nose. It was where the trunk attached to the elephant's face.

1. Another title for this story might be
   - **a.** "The Cyclops."
   - **b.** "A Terrifying Nose."
   - **c.** "Stories from Today."
   - **d.** "An Elephant."
2. What is **not** true about the cyclops?
   - **a.** It is a giant.
   - **b.** It has one eye.
   - **c.** It is real.
   - **d.** Stories are told about it.
3. A *synonym* is a word that means the same thing as another word. What word from the story is a synonym for *middle*?
   - **a.** huge
   - **b.** center
   - **c.** truth
   - **d.** opening
4. From the story, you can tell that
   - **a.** all stories are from long ago.
   - **b.** all stories are made up.
   - **c.** some stories are made up.
   - **d.** no stories are from long ago.
5. Most likely, the author wrote this story
   - **a.** to terrify you.
   - **b.** to tell you how some stories started.
   - **c.** to teach you all about skulls.
   - **d.** to make you think about your eyes.

Name: jaYla

Some Kind of Giant

"Are you sure that it's safe to go out?" Zeepa asked Zoopa.

"As long as we stay attached to the ship with our breathing tubes, we will be fine," Zoopa assured Zeepa. "Come on!"

"I like this green stuff we're moving through," Zeepa started to say. She never finished her sentence because something was coming toward them. It was huge! It seemed to block the sky. Nearer and nearer it came. It was so big that it was making the ground shake!

"It's some kind of a giant!" Zoopa cried. "We've got to get out of here. Back to the ship as fast as you can!"

Zeepa and Zoopa rushed to the ship. They rolled to the driving deck and pushed the button for take-off. With a *buzz*, they lifted up and began their journey home. Soaring into the air, they went past the giant's face. "It has two eyes," Zoopa cried in wonder, "and only one nose!"

"I'm glad I'm not an Earthling," Zeepa said. "I can't imagine only having two eyes and one nose!"

1. What hint does the author give that Zoopa and Zeepa may not have legs?
   a. When they went to the driving deck, they rolled.
   b. When they left the ship, they had breathing tubes.
   c. When they took off, they pushed a button.
   d. When they began their journey home, they could not see.

2. Most likely, the green stuff Zeepa liked was
   a. water. b. grass. c. a lime. d. peas.

3. Another title for this story might be
   a. "Zeepa and Zoopa Find a Friend."
   b. "Earthling Steps on Aliens."
   c. "How the Alien Ship Flew."
   d. "What Scared the Aliens?"

4. Why did the author make you wait to find out that Zoopa and Zeepa are very small?
   a. She wanted you to be surprised at the end.
   b. She didn't think it was an important part of the story.
   c. She wanted you to be scared at the end.
   d. She wanted you to think Zoopa and Zeepa were giants.

5. Most likely, Zeepa and Zoopa
   a. are from Earth. b. can breathe air. c. are very small. d. have two eyes.

Name: ______________________________

Write On!

Explain how Sam could have mistaken an elephant for a submarine periscope. Use information from “Snorkeling” and “The Periscope” in your answer.

Next, tell why it is easy for an elephant to hold its trunk out of the water for long periods of time. Use information from “A Fable About Wishing” in your answer.

Name: ______________________________

A Great Gymnast

Simone Biles won. She won again and again. She won world championships. She won Olympic gold medals. None of it came easily. Biles had to work hard on her skills. She had to train for hours every day. All of Biles's hard work in the gym paid off. Today, she is one of the world's greatest gymnasts.

Biles can leap high off a four-inch beam. She can twist two and a half times in the air. When she comes down to the ground, she does not fall. She lands perfectly.

One of Biles's coaches had a message for her. The message was, "Focus on your talent—not your failures." Biles's mother also had a message for her. Biles's mother told her, "We're your family—not your fans. You don't get any special treatment here."

1. If Biles did all the things below, which one would her coach tell her to focus on?
   - **a.** not getting a medal
   - **b.** falling off a beam
   - **c.** landing perfectly
   - **d.** losing a championship

2. Biles is one of the world's greatest gymnasts because
   - **a.** she can leap off a beam.
   - **b.** she got special treatment.
   - **c.** she went to the gym.
   - **d.** she trained and worked hard.

3. From the story, you can tell that at home, Biles most likely
   - **a.** made big messes.
   - **b.** helped her family.
   - **c.** left dirty dishes in every room.
   - **d.** thought other people should do her work.

4. When you *focus* on something, you
   - **a.** pay attention to it or think about it a lot.
   - **b.** don't pay attention to it or don't think about it at all.
   - **c.** go to the gym and do two and a half twists.
   - **d.** don't go to the gym or don't do any twists.

Name: ______________________________

Fast, Faster, Fastest

Anna said, "I'm fast. I'm so fast I can beat a tortoise in every race."

Marta said, "You may be fast, but I'm faster. I can beat a tortoise and a dog in every race."

Jinjing said, "You are both fast, but I can go faster. I can beat a tortoise and a dog in a race. I can also beat a horse!"

Sasha said, "A cheetah is the fastest animal. I can run faster than a cheetah, so no one can beat me in a race."

Kelsey didn't boast or say how fast she was. She simply said, "It's time to go to sleep." Then she blew out the candle and jumped into bed. Kelsey was under the covers before the room got dark!

1. In the story, who is fastest?
   - **a.** Anna
   - **b.** Marta
   - **c.** Jinjing
   - **d.** Kelsey

2. How do you know which girl was the fastest?
   - **a.** She said she was the fastest.
   - **b.** She moved faster than light.
   - **c.** She said she could beat a cheetah.
   - **d.** She won every race.

3. Put the animals in order from slowest to fastest.
   - **a.** tortoise, dog, cheetah, horse
   - **b.** cheetah, horse, dog, tortoise
   - **c.** tortoise, dog, horse, cheetah
   - **d.** dog, tortoise, horse, cheetah

4. This story
   - **a.** is true.
   - **b.** is fiction.
   - **c.** is about six girls.
   - **d.** is about the dark.

Name: ______________________________

Sonic Boom

An airplane is flying over at 750 miles per hour. That is faster than the speed of sound! What do we hear down on the ground? We hear a sonic boom. A sonic boom sounds like a small explosion. We may hear the sonic boom anywhere from 2 to 60 seconds after flyover.

Planes and rockets can make sonic booms. There is something else that can break the sound barrier and make a sonic boom, too. It was something that was invented a long time ago. It can't be driven or flown, and it doesn't even have a motor. It is something you can hold. What could it possibly be?

It is a bullwhip! The end of the whip can move faster than the speed of sound. When it does, it cracks! The crack is the sound of a sonic boom.

1. When is a sonic boom heard?
   - **a.** when a plane is flying over at 450 miles per hour
   - **b.** 60 minutes after flyover
   - **c.** when eggs are whipped
   - **d.** when something travels faster than the speed of sound
2. From the story, you can tell that the crack of a whip sounds like
   - **a.** a big bell.
   - **b.** a small explosion.
   - **c.** a motor.
   - **d.** a rocket when it lands.
3. What does it mean when we say "break the sound barrier"?
   - **a.** It means that something went faster than the speed of sound.
   - **b.** It means that people have invented something.
   - **c.** It means that that someone drove something with a motor.
   - **d.** It means that a plane or rocket exploded.
4. Which of the following is least likely to make a sonic boom?
   - **a.** a jet
   - **b.** a rocket
   - **c.** a school bus
   - **d.** lightning

Name: ______________________________

Closing the Gap

The race was on! Abel Mutai from Kenya was a great runner. In the Olympic Games, he had won a medal. Now, he was going to win this race, too! He was ahead of everyone. No other runner was close to him. He would surely win! Then, something happened.

Mutai made a mistake. He stopped too soon. He thought he had crossed the finish line. Everyone was yelling at him. They were all telling him to cross the finish line. Mutai didn't! Why didn't Mutai cross the line? The race was in Spain. Mutai didn't know Spanish! He couldn't understand what people were yelling at him.

Ivan Fernandez Anaya caught up to Mutai. He could have passed Mutai, but he didn't. Instead, Anaya stayed behind Mutai while guiding him to the finish line. Anaya said, "I didn't deserve to win it. I did what I had to do. He was the rightful winner. He created a gap that I couldn't have closed if he hadn't made a mistake."

1. From the story, you can tell that, in Kenya,
- **a.** some people do not speak Spanish.
- **b.** people don't do what they are told if they are yelled at.
- **c.** no one has ever gone to the Olympic Games.
- **d.** runners don't care about crossing the finish line.

2. A *gap* is
- **a.** a hole or a space between two things.
- **b.** a person who shows you how to do something.
- **c.** a mistake or something you did wrong.
- **d.** a thing you deserve or have won.

3. From the story, you can tell that
- **a.** Anaya had never won a medal before.
- **b.** Anaya had lost to Mutai in the Olympic Games.
- **c.** Anaya was faster than Mutai.
- **d.** Anaya could have won the race if he wanted to.

4. This story is mainly about
- **a.** races in Kenya and Spain.
- **b.** a runner who helped another runner.
- **c.** why people yelled at a race.
- **d.** how to cross a finish line.

5. What statement do you think Anaya would agree with the most?
- **a.** Winning is everything.
- **b.** Medals are the only thing that matters.
- **c.** The fastest people always win.
- **d.** Someone else's mistake should not make you a winner.

Name: ______________________________

Charlie and Dill

Charlie Cheetah was showing off. "I'm the fastest!" he gloated. "I win every race!" All the animals were tired of Charlie's boasting. They didn't like it, but Charlie was the fastest. What could they do?

Dill Armadillo said, "Three days from now, I will race you." The day of the race, Charlie took off like wildfire. He was out of sight before Dill had gone more than few yards.

Charlie ran up to the first checkpoint. Dill was already there! Charlie ran up to the second checkpoint. Dill was already there! Charlie ran up to the third checkpoint. Dill was already there! Charlie ran to the finish line. Dill was just crossing it!

Charlie didn't boast. He didn't gloat. He slunk away with his head down. Dill waited. He waited for his first brother. He waited for his second brother. He waited for his third brother. All the brothers were identical. They looked exactly the same. Charlie didn't know something. He didn't know that nine-banded armadillos always give birth to four identical young.

1. Most likely, Dill wanted to wait three days to race so that
   - a. he could have time to rest.
   - b. his brothers could get to the checkpoints.
   - c. the other animals could see the race.
   - d. Charlie would have time to slink away.

2. This story is mainly about
   - a. the fastest animal.
   - b. identical animals.
   - c. an animal that was tricked.
   - d. animals at checkpoints.

3. *Gloating* is another word for
   - a. boasting.
   - b. running.
   - c. losing.
   - d. racing.

4. How do you know Charlie felt bad at the end of the race?
   - a. He raced away with his head up.
   - b. He raced away with his head down.
   - c. He slunk away with his head up.
   - d. He slunk away with his head down.

5. When it said that Charlie "took off like wildfire," it meant
   - a. that Charlie was on fire.
   - b. that a wildfire had started.
   - c. that Charlie went fast like a fire.
   - d. that Dill might get burned.

Name: ______________________________

Write On!

Think about the stories "Closing the Gap" and "Charlie and Dill." Compare and contrast the two stories. Tell how they are alike. Tell how they are different.

Then, tell what advice you think Ivan Fernandez Anaya would give to Dill. Last, tell what advice you think Simone Biles would give to Charlie.

Name: ______________________________

Hero Dogs

Children were sick. Medicine was needed. A doctor warned, "Children will die. I need medicine." How could the doctor get the medicine? The doctor was in Nome. Nome is a town in Alaska. It was winter. The year was 1924. The only way to get to Nome was by dogsled.

The medicine was far away. The usual dogsled delivery time took 25 days. That was too late. The medicine would not work after six days. Could the dogs do it? Could they get to Nome in just six days?

Temperatures dropped to more than 50 degrees below zero. Winds raged at 80 miles per hour. Mushers were so blinded by snow that they couldn't even see their dogs! The dogs pulled and pulled. They never stopped. The dogs were heroes. They saved the children.

1. This story is mainly about
   - a. the temperature in Alaska.
   - b. how dogs saved children.
   - c. how children get sick.
   - d. how to get to Nome.
2. From the story, you can tell that a *musher* is most likely
   - a. a person who likes mush.
   - b. a dog who helps pull a sled.
   - c. a person who drives a dogsled.
   - d. a child who needs medicine.
3. Why did the dogs have to go so fast?
   - a. The medicine would not work after six days.
   - b. It was winter.
   - c. It was more than 50 degrees below zero.
   - d. More than 80 children were sick.
4. What did the author mean when she said that the wind *raged*?
   - a. It blew very softly.
   - b. It blew very hard.
   - c. It blew very gently.
   - d. It blew very quietly.

Name: ______________________________

Moose Alley

The part of the trail called "Moose Alley" was coming up. Brenda looked carefully to the left and to the right. She didn't want a moose to hurt her dogs. Last year, a moose had kicked one of her dogs so hard that the dog landed in a tree!

What kind of race was Brenda in? It was a dogsledding race. The race is called the *Iditarod*, and it is over 1,000 miles long. It takes place once a year. Back in 1924, dogs had carried medicine to Nome, Alaska. The race took place on the same trail.

Brenda made it safely through Moose Alley. Then, she stopped the sled. "Time to change your boots," she said to the dogs. "You don't have to wear boots because it is cold. You have to wear boots to protect your footpads."

1. The part of the trail called "Moose Alley" most likely received its name because
- **a.** it is like a small street.
- **b.** it is part of the Iditarod trail.
- **c.** it is a place where dogs need boots.
- **d.** it is a place where moose are often seen.

2. Most likely, the dogs needed boots because
- **a.** it was so cold.
- **b.** they helped protect them from moose.
- **c.** the trail was icy and rocky.
- **d.** they made it easier to kick a moose.

3. What fact about the Iditarod do you know to be true from reading the story?
- **a.** It began after 1924.
- **b.** It began before 1924.
- **c.** It started in 1924.
- **d.** It has only been run one time since 1924.

4. From the story, you can tell that the Iditarod
- **a.** is an easy and fun race.
- **b.** takes place when it is warm.
- **c.** is on a paved road through small towns.
- **d.** is a very hard and dangerous race.

Name: ______________________________

Dangerous Ice

Peter banged his pole on the ice. Over and over again, he tested it. It looked firm, so Peter stepped forward. Suddenly, the ice collapsed! Peter sank into the icy water. He was completely submerged!

Peter tried and tried to get out. He couldn't. The ice kept breaking off. Peter knew he had to get out. No one was there to help him. There were no dogs to pull him. In a few more seconds, Peter would be too cold to move.

Peter was in a special race. The race followed the Iditarod Trail. Peter had to go 1,000 miles in 30 days. Peter needed to run on some parts of the trail, ski on other parts, and ride a fat-tired bike on another part.

Finally, Peter heaved himself out of the ice water and onto the solid ice. Peter knew that if he didn't start moving, he would freeze to death. He had to move to stay warm. Pulling his sled behind him, Peter didn't stop running until the next checkpoint.

1. This story is mainly about
   - **a.** a dangerous race.
   - **b.** a dogsled race.
   - **c.** skiing for 30 days.
   - **d.** swimming in cold water.

2. When something is *firm*, it is
   - **a.** thin and weak.
   - **b.** strong and stable.
   - **c.** cold and icy.
   - **d.** loose and wobbly.

3. Why was it hard for Peter to get out of the water?
   - **a.** He couldn't reach the ice.
   - **b.** The ice was too slippery.
   - **c.** The ice kept breaking off.
   - **d.** The ice was too thick.

4. From the story, you can tell that Peter
   - **a.** likes warm places.
   - **b.** doesn't know how to swim.
   - **c.** likes to run more than he likes to bike.
   - **d.** doesn't give up easily.

Name: ______________________________

Stove Sitting

Someone tells you that they sit on a stove. Did you hear right? Is the person pulling your leg? Yes, you heard correctly. No, the person is not trying to trick you. The person did say that they sit on a stove. Why in the world would someone sit on a stove?

Racers in the Iditarod have teams of 16 dogs. The dogs work very hard to pull the sled. They use up lots of energy. They may eat over 10 times what they usually eat. On the trail, the dogs get frozen snacks. They might get chunks of fish, meat, or soaked dog food.

There are several checkpoints on the race. At the checkpoints, the mushers cook warm meals for their dogs. They make up a slurry, or thick mixture, for the dogs. The slurry may be made up of beef, fish, vitamins, dog food, and chicken fat. The slurry is cooked in a bucket camp stove. What is the bucket camp stove used for when it is not being used to cook? It is the driver's seat on the sled!

1. What is **not** part of the slurry?
   - a. fish
   - b. vitamins
   - c. chicken fat
   - d. bread

2. In the story, what does "pulling your leg" mean?
   - a. It means that someone is tricking you.
   - b. It means that someone is pulling on your leg.
   - c. It means that someone is sitting on a stove.
   - d. It means that someone is not hearing correctly.

3. Most likely, the musher sits on the stove
   - a. to stay warm.
   - b. to keep it from falling off the sled.
   - c. to save space.
   - d. to keep the food safe.

4. This story is mainly about
   - a. different places to sit.
   - b. how one thing can have two uses.
   - c. how people cook outside.
   - d. good snacks.

5. You find out why someone sits on a stove
   - a. when you read the title.
   - b. when you read the first paragraph.
   - c. when you read the second paragraph.
   - d. when you read the last paragraph.

Name: ______________________________

What Word?

When my musher says, "Hike!" I know what to do. "Hike" is the command to get moving. When my musher wants me to turn left, he says, "Haw!" When my musher says, "Gee!" I turn right. I'm the lead dog because I pull hard and listen carefully.

It didn't take me long at all to learn all the command words. My musher says, "Easy!" when he wants me to slow down. He says, "Whoa!" when he wants me to stop. When we have to go by another team or anything else that might distract us, my musher yells, "On by!" That command means "Pay attention! Just stay on task and follow directions!"

One time, Marshall collapsed on the trail. This was during the 2012 Iditarod. Marshall was a swing dog and a strong puller, so I was very surprised. What did my musher do? He did something I have never seen or witnessed before. He put his mouth on Marshall's snout! He breathed in and out! He saved Marshall's life. Is there a word for mouth-to-snout breathing?

1. Who tells this story?
   - **a.** a musher
   - **b.** Marshall
   - **c.** a lead dog
   - **d.** a swing dog

2. This story is fiction (made up), but it is full of facts. What answer is **not** a fact?
   - **a.** The command for right is "Gee!"
   - **b.** A musher once saved his dog Marshall by breathing into his snout.
   - **c.** There are lead dogs and swing dogs.
   - **d.** I think sled dogs do not like to run.

3. If you *witness* something, you
   - **a.** command it.
   - **b.** see it.
   - **c.** collapse.
   - **d.** get distracted.

4. While passing another dog team, if the musher wants her team to stay focused on the trail, she might yell out
   - **a.** "On by!"
   - **b.** "Haw!"
   - **c.** "Easy!"
   - **d.** "Hike!"

5. When something *falls down* or *apart,* it
   - **a.** collapses.
   - **b.** pays attention.
   - **c.** listens carefully.
   - **d.** stays on task.

Name: ______________________________

Write On!

Use information from the stories to describe the Iditarod Sled Race. Tell how the race started.

Then tell what might happen to a musher, a dog, and a person running the race.

Musher: ______________________________

____

____

____

Dog: ______________________________

____

____

____

Person: ______________________________

____

____

____

Finally, pick a musher, a dog, or a person running the race. Which would you rather be and why?

____

____

____

____

Name: ____________________

A Rule for Walls

A hotel is a place where you pay for a safe place to sleep. You may stay one night, two nights, or more. Many people stay in hotels when they are taking a trip or traveling on vacation.

There is a hotel in Bolivia with a rule. The rule is about the walls. The rule is that you can't lick the walls. Why does the hotel in Bolivia have this rule? The walls will fall apart! They will disintegrate!

Why will the walls fall apart? Why will they disintegrate if you lick them? The walls are made of salt. The entire hotel is made of salt. The tables, beds, chairs, and floor are made of salt. Where is this hotel? It is in the middle of the world's largest salt flat.

1. When something *disintegrates,*
   - **a.** it is licked.
   - **b.** it falls apart.
   - **c.** it is in Bolivia.
   - **d.** it is made of salt.

2. This story was written
   - **a.** to make you want to stay in a hotel.
   - **b.** to show you what you can do with salt.
   - **c.** to tell you about a hotel in Bolivia.
   - **d.** to teach you to follow rules.

3. Who would most likely stay in a hotel?
   - **a.** a zebra on a vacation
   - **b.** a teacher who had to go to a meeting far away
   - **c.** a doctor who walked to work
   - **d.** an astronaut up in space

4. An *antonym* is a word that means the opposite of another word. What word is an antonym for *apart*?

   a. chair   **b.** happy   **c.** sleep   **d.** together

Name: ______________________________

What Glowed in the Dark?

"There!" Noah cried. "There it is again!" He pointed to the west, and this time Anna saw what Noah was talking about. Little glowing lights were moving across the ground.

When Noah and Anna saw the lights coming toward them, they raced back to their hotel. Their hotel was in a cave. It had been dug out of the ground. Most of the houses, churches, and restaurants in Coober Pedy were also in caves. This was because it was cool underground. Above ground, it was often over 100 degrees.

Noah and Anna reported the strange lights. They were told, "Don't worry. In this part of Australia, it's too hot to play golf in the daytime. We play at night instead with balls that glow."

1. Why did people play with balls that glowed?
   - a. They rolled better.
   - b. They were cooler.
   - c. They liked the color.
   - d. They were easy to see.
2. This story is mainly about
   - a. what two children saw.
   - b. Australia.
   - c. cave living.
   - d. how to play golf.
3. Why is the title "What Glowed in the Dark?" a better title than "Golf Balls That Glowed"?
   - a. The first title makes you think about golf.
   - b. The second title doesn't tell you about caves.
   - c. The first title lets you be surprised.
   - d. The second title makes you think of Australia.
4. Most likely, the town of Coober Pedy
   - a. is in a forest.
   - b. is in the desert.
   - c. is in the Arctic.
   - d. is in North America.

Name: ______________________________

A Long Sleep

Ursa yawned. Oh, she was so tired. She curled up on her bed after finding the most comfortable spot. Her eyes closed, and she fell into a deep sleep. The snow piled up all around Ursa's home, but Ursa didn't notice.

Ursa's heart slowed. For every three times it used to beat, now it only beat once. She didn't eat or drink. She didn't even go to the bathroom! How long did this go on? It went on for five months! It would be impossible for you to go five months without eating. How was it possible for Ursa?

Ursa was a bear! Food is hard to find in winter months. Bears survive by going into a state of hibernation. Most people think bears are starving when they wake up. The truth is that it may take a week or two after waking up before bears start feeling really hungry.

1. When do you find out that Ursa is a bear?
   - **a.** before you are told she didn't eat
   - **b.** before you are told she didn't notice the snow
   - **c.** before you are told her heart slowed
   - **d.** before you are told she was in a state of hibernation

2. How long can a bear go without eating?
   - **a.** 5 days
   - **b.** 5 months
   - **c.** 9 days
   - **d.** 9 months

3. If something *can't be done*, it
   - **a.** is impossible.
   - **b.** can't be noticed.
   - **c.** is comfortable.
   - **d.** can't be hungry.

4. Bears go into a state of hibernation because
   - **a.** it is better for their hearts not to beat so fast.
   - **b.** they do not like playing in the snow.
   - **c.** it is hard to find food in the winter months.
   - **d.** they can do impossible things.

Name: ______________________________

When the Sun Sets

Most people go to sleep soon after the sun sets. They get up soon after the sun rises. There are some people who don't do this. The sun sets, and they keep working. The sun rises and sets again, and they keep working! They keep working even after the sun has risen many times! How do they do this? Aren't they tired? Don't they need to go to sleep?

The people are astronauts. They are on the International Space Station. High above us, they are circling Earth. Here on Earth, a day lasts 24 hours. We see the sun set and rise one time every 24 hours. It is different for the astronauts. In 24 hours, they see 16 sunsets and 16 sunrises!

The astronauts don't sleep on beds. The beds would float away. The astronauts get in bags. They attach the bags to a wall. If they don't strap down their arms, something happens. Their arms float up into the air!

1. When you *strap something down*, you

a. attach it. **b.** circle it. **c.** float it. **d.** see it.

2. Why might it be hard for an astronaut to know when it is time to sleep?

a. An astronaut's day is longer than 24 hours.
b. There are 16 sunsets in 24 hours.
c. He or she doesn't have a bed to sleep in.
d. All the clocks have floated away.

3. If an astronaut has long hair and doesn't tie it down before sleeping, what might happen?

a. None of the hairs would move.
b. Some of the hairs would get wet.
c. Most of the hairs would stay flat.
d. All the hairs would float up into the air.

4. What would happen to you if you waited for 16 sunsets before falling asleep?

a. You would be fine.
b. You would not be hungry.
c. You would not be tired.
d. You would not be able to think right.

5. Another title for this story might be

a. "When Astronauts Sleep."
b. "Sleeping in Sleeping Bags."
c. "All About the International Space Station."
d. "Why a Day Is 24 Hours."

Name: ____

The Missing Hotel

Molly wanted to stay in the Ice Hotel in Sweden. The entire hotel was made of ice. The walls, beds, chairs, and tables were made of ice. Even the cups were made of ice! "You sleep on reindeer furs," Molly told Lewis. "And you have to dress warmly because it never gets above freezing."

Molly and Lewis decided to go to Sweden in July. They rented a car and drove to the city with the Ice Hotel. They looked and looked, but they couldn't find the hotel. "Where can it be?" Molly asked in a worried tone. "How can a huge hotel with 100 rooms disappear? This is a nightmare!"

Molly and Lewis were not in the wrong place. They were in the right place but at the wrong time. They had come in the summer. The hotel wasn't there because it had melted!

"You'll have to come back," Molly and Lewis were told. "We build a new Ice Hotel every year. You just have to come between December and April."

1. What kind of furs do visitors to the Ice Hotel sleep on?
   a. fox furs **b.** polar bear furs **c.** reindeer furs **d.** rabbit furs

2. When Molly said, "This is a nightmare!" what did she mean?
   a. She was surprised at what she had dreamed.
   b. She had never gone to Sweden.
   c. She wanted to wake up and stop dreaming.
   d. She felt as if she were having a bad dream.

3. The next time Molly and Lewis go to see the Ice Hotel, when should they go?
   a. January **b.** June **c.** August **d.** September

4. What should Molly and Lewis have checked before they left for Sweden?
   a. when the hotel was open
   b. where the hotel was
   c. what temperature it was in the hotel
   d. why the chairs were made of ice

5. If someone told you that they had stayed in Sweden's Ice Hotel for five years, you would know that
   a. they had the same room each year.
   b. they stayed for the entire five years.
   c. they had a different room each year.
   d. they came at the same time as Molly and Lewis.

Name: ______________________________

Write On!

Choose a setting from one of the stories in Unit 4 and pretend that you must sleep there for a week. Write a letter to a friend explaining some of the positive and negative experiences of your visit.

Name: Jayla 7.11.21 100 A+

Joey for Dinner?

A dingo is after a kangaroo! The wild animal is getting closer! The kangaroo hops as fast as it can. Is it fast enough to get away from the dingo? No, it is not! The dingo is catching up!

In the middle of a hop, high in the air, the kangaroo does something. What does she do? She releases her joey from her pouch. It lands in some tall grass. Is the mother kangaroo abandoning her baby? Is she going to let her joey be eaten?

The mother kangaroo is much lighter now. She can go faster. She can hop farther. She leads the dingo away from her baby. Now, the mother kangaroo is too fast for the dingo. The dingo gives up. The mother kangaroo does not abandon her baby. She picks it up when it is safe to do so.

1. When you *abandon* something, you
   - **a.** leave it somewhere.
   - **b.** chase it.
   - **c.** keep it safe.
   - **d.** eat it.
2. Why was the mother kangaroo able to go faster?
   - **a.** She didn't want the dingo to catch her.
   - **b.** She had her baby in her pouch.
   - **c.** She was lighter.
   - **d.** She was running in tall grass.
3. From the story, you can tell that a baby kangaroo is called
   - **a.** a *dingo*.
   - **b.** a *roo*.
   - **c.** a *kitten*.
   - **d.** a *joey*.
4. From the story, you can tell that the mother kangaroo dropped her baby into the tall grass because
   - **a.** she liked jumping high.
   - **b.** she cared about it.
   - **c.** she was tired of it.
   - **d.** she wanted the dingo to find it.

Name: Jayla

The Strange Pouch

Some big, mean emu scares my mother, and what does my mother do? She tosses me out and hops off. I understand. She was terrified, and I know she wanted to weigh as little as possible so she could make a fast getaway. I'm just wondering how long I have to wait for her.

How did it get to be so dark? I must have fallen asleep. Oh, there's a pouch. I'll just jump right in! Ouch, ouch, yuck! What is in this thing? I'm getting poked and jabbed by things that have edges and sharp points! This is one strange pouch!

Oh, no! I'm being lifted up and placed onto someone's back! Now I know something is really wrong because every kangaroo knows that pouches are supposed to go in front. Pouches go on bellies, not on backs!

1. The strange pouch is most likely a
   a. purse. **b.** paper bag. **c.** backpack. **d.** suitcase.
2. Which sentence best sums up the story?
   a. The story is about a mean emu.
   b. The story is about a kangaroo that is chased by an emu.
   c. The story is about a joey that falls asleep.
   d. The story is about a joey that gets in the wrong pouch.
3. A *synonym* is a word that means the same thing as another word. What word is a synonym for *scared*?
   a. terrified **b.** poked **c.** wondering **d.** tossed
4. Most likely, how does the kangaroo in the pouch feel at the end of the story?
   a. upset **b.** happy **c.** glad **d.** sleepy

Name: ______________________________

Hero Kangaroo

Sydney News

HERO KANGAROO

By **John Kelly**

Doug March was saved by an unlikely hero. Lulu is a one-eyed kangaroo. March had found Lulu when she was still a joey. She was sick, but March nursed her back to health. "She had been abandoned," March said. "She can't see well, so we kept her around the place."

March lives on a sheep farm. He had gone out to check on his flock after last night's storm. A huge limb that had been weakened by the wind broke and fell on him. Lulu was with him.

"Lulu stood over him and barked and barked," Julie said. "My dad wasn't moving, so she knew something was wrong. She wouldn't leave him. She just kept barking until someone came. My dad once saved Lulu, but today Lulu saved my dad. Lulu is a true hero."

1. What did Doug March do for a living?
   - a. He cut down trees.
   - b. He was a nurse.
   - c. He was a vet.
   - d. He was a sheep farmer.
2. From the story, you can tell that a group of sheep is called a
   - a. flock.
   - b. herd.
   - c. litter.
   - d. mob.
3. How did Lulu save Doug March?
   - a. by pushing a limb off him
   - b. by making noise until someone came
   - c. by nursing him back to health
   - d. by keeping the sheep away from him
4. A *proverb* is a short, wise saying. What proverb fits this story?
   - a. A watched pot never boils.
   - b. Do good, and good will come to you.
   - c. All good things must come to an end.
   - d. A picture is worth a thousand words.

Name: ____________________

Unlikely Friends

Two baby marsupials share a pouch. Marsupials are special kinds of mammals. They have pouches. The baby marsupials hug each other. They groom each other. They suck on each other's ears. They sleep together. The baby marsupials are the best of friends. One of the babies will grow very big. It will be able to hop. One will grow to be the size of a small pig. It will not be able to hop. How can they share a pouch?

Anzac is a kangaroo. His mother was hit by a car. Anzac was found inside his mother's pouch. He was brought to a Wildlife Animal Center. Anzac needed to go back inside a pouch. Peggy is a wombat. Her mother had been hit by a car, too. Peggy also needed a pouch. Workers at the Wildlife Animal Center made a pouch for Peggy. When Anzac came, they put him in the same pouch.

One of the workers said, "They feel each other's heartbeats. They comfort each other. They are good for each other."

1. How do marsupials differ from other mammals?
   - **a.** They have ears.
   - **b.** They can be big.
   - **c.** They have pouches.
   - **d.** They can hop.
2. Most likely, what did the author want you to learn from this story?
   - **a.** It is not good to share.
   - **b.** Marsupials are the best kinds of mammals.
   - **c.** Wombats and kangaroos can hop.
   - **d.** Friends come in all shapes and sizes.
3. If you *comfort* someone, you
   - **a.** make them feel better.
   - **b.** take them out of a pouch.
   - **c.** are a special kind of mammal.
   - **d.** feel their ears.
4. Which happened first in the Wildlife Animal Center?
   - **a.** Anzac was brought to the Wildlife Animal Center.
   - **b.** Anzac felt Peggy's heartbeat.
   - **c.** Peggy was brought to the Wildlife Animal Center.
   - **d.** Peggy hugged Anzac.
5. Most likely, when Anzac and Peggy shared a pouch,
   - **a.** Anzac was much bigger than Peggy.
   - **b.** Anzac and Peggy were about the same size.
   - **c.** Anzac was much smaller than Peggy.
   - **d.** Anzac was one year older than Peggy.

Name: ____________________________________

Surprise Answers

Izzy went to the zoo along with her class. Izzy liked the kangaroo exhibit the best. The rest of Izzy's class moved on to see the bears, but Izzy lagged behind. She was about to leave when she heard a voice.

"Little girl," the voice said. "Are there any questions I can answer?" Izzy looked around. Her classmates were out of sight. Who could be talking to her? "It's me," the voice said. "The kangaroo right in front of you. I'm very wise. Ask me anything you want."

Izzy had two questions. She wanted to know when kangaroos stopped growing. She also wanted to know how high kangaroos could jump. The first answer surprised her. She was told that kangaroos never stop growing! The second answer surprised her, too. She was told kangaroos can jump high. How high? Higher than the tallest skyscraper!

Izzy asked if she was being told the truth. The kangaroo said, "Yes. Kangaroos never stop growing. Most mammals do, but we don't."

"That's fascinating," said Izzy. "But you can't really jump higher than the tallest skyscraper, can you?"

"Of course I can," the kangaroo replied. "Skyscrapers can't jump!"

1. This story is fiction. It is made up, but it has facts in it. What fact is in the story?
   - **a.** Kangaroos can talk.
   - **b.** Kangaroos never stop growing.
   - **c.** Kangaroos can answer questions.
   - **d.** Kangaroos jump over skyscrapers.

2. If you *lag behind*, you
   - **a.** go in front.
   - **b.** fall behind.
   - **c.** go fast.
   - **d.** fall asleep.

3. This story is mainly about
   - **a.** a class trip to the zoo.
   - **b.** how kangaroos are mammals.
   - **c.** a kangaroo who answered two questions.
   - **d.** what zoo exhibit a girl liked best.

4. Why didn't anyone else hear the kangaroo's voice?
   - **a.** They were all at the bird exhibit.
   - **b.** They were all at the snake exhibit.
   - **c.** They were all at the camel exhibit.
   - **d.** They were all at the bear exhibit.

5. Most likely, if you asked the wise kangaroo what a kangaroo's favorite game is, he would answer
   - **a.** jump rope.
   - **b.** baseball.
   - **c.** basketball.
   - **d.** soccer.

Name: ____________________

Write On!

Write a newspaper article about an abandoned kangaroo. Your story will be fiction, but you must include the following words in your story: *joey, marsupial, pouch,* and *dingo*.

____

Newspaper name

____

Title of article

Name: ____________________

The Open Window

Alexander Fleming was a scientist. In the 1920s, he did something. It was a small thing, but it made a big thing happen. Fleming took the lid off of a dish. A window was open, and some mold from a plant blew in. It landed in the dish. Fleming did not throw the dish away. He thought, "I will see what happens."

A new green mold began to grow. Nothing would grow around the mold. Fleming thought, "This mold is powerful. It could help people. It could kill bacteria." Other scientists put the mold into a new form. It was a form that people could use. They called it *penicillin*. Scientists learned to make many forms of penicillin. All the drugs were made from green or blue molds. An open window changed medicine forever!

1. What blew in the open window?
   - a. leaf mold
   - b. blue mold
   - c. plant mold
   - d. green mold

2. You could sum up this story by saying that
   - a. it is about why we should leave windows open.
   - b. it is about the life of Alexander Fleming.
   - c. it is about discovering a new drug.
   - d. it is about how molds can hurt us.

3. A *synonym* is a word that means the same thing as another word. A synonym for *powerful* is
   - a. strong.
   - b. happy.
   - c. big.
   - d. lucky.

4. From the story, you can tell that
   - a. five scientists helped to make penicillin.
   - b. more than one scientist helped to make penicillin.
   - c. 20 scientists helped to make penicillin.
   - d. Fleming was the only scientist who helped make penicillin.

Name: ______________________________

All Wrong

Linda was going to the aquarium. Linda was glad that she would see fish. She was glad that she would see sharks. What made her happiest of all was that she was going to see a green sea turtle. "All my life, I have wanted to see a bright-green sea turtle," Linda said.

At the aquarium, Linda raced to the green sea turtle tank. Linda saw a lot of turtles. She saw turtles that had brown shells. She saw turtles that had black shells. She saw turtles that had olive shells, but she did not see any bright-green turtles. "Something is all wrong!" she cried. "The green turtles are missing!"

A worker said, "Green sea turtles have brown, black, or olive-colored shells. They are called 'green sea turtles' because their fat is green."

1. Most likely, what other things would Linda see at an aquarium?
   a. monkeys b. sea stars c. horses d. elephants
2. You can tell that Linda really wanted to see the green sea turtles because
   a. she raced to their tank.
   b. she asked the worker where their tank was.
   c. she walked to their tank.
   d. she stayed at their tank for a long time.
3. Most likely, how did Linda feel at the end of the story?
   a. hungry b. tired c. afraid d. surprised
4. Linda saw turtles that had all but what color shell?
   a. olive b. orange c. black d. brown

Name: ______________________________

Riddle Play

Setting: Inside a second-grade classroom

Cast: Teacher: Ms. Allen

Students: Miguel, Sophie, Karen, Brendan, Brad, Lexie, Roger

Miguel: There was a green house. Inside the green house, there was a white house. Inside the white house, there was a red house. Inside the red house, there were a lot of babies. What am I thinking of?

Ms. Allen: Does anyone know the answer to Miguel's riddle?

Sophie: I think that Miguel should give us another hint.

Miguel: It is something that you can eat.

Karen: I know! I know! It's a watermelon! Now it's my turn. When do you go on red and stop on green?

Brendan: I think Karen should give us another hint.

Karen: It has something to do with what you can eat.

Brad: I know! I know! When you are eating a watermelon!

A bell rings.

Lexie and Roger: That bell rang just in time. All that talk about watermelon made us hungry!

1. Most likely, the babies in Miguel's riddle
   - a. are the green watermelon rind.
   - b. want to stay inside the house.
   - c. are the part of the watermelon you eat.
   - d. are the watermelon seeds.
2. Who said that Karen should give another hint?
   - a. Brendan
   - b. Lexie
   - c. Miguel
   - d. Sophie
3. When writing a play, the author includes the setting
   - a. so you can feel as if you are at school.
   - b. so you can know what people say.
   - c. so you know where the play takes place.
   - d. so you will know how long the play is.
4. This play would have been hard to understand if you
   - a. did not like riddles.
   - b. did not know what a bell sounded like.
   - c. had never seen or eaten a watermelon.
   - d. were not hungry.

Name: ____________________

Bee Thrashing

Wham! The bee is slammed down on the branch. Over and over, the bee is slammed down. It is getting a real thrashing! Why is the bee being beaten? Why is it being thrashed?

There is a bird called the *green bee-eater*. It is found in parts of Africa and Asia. The green bee-eater sits on a perch. Its perch can be a wire or a branch. It looks all around, searching for prey. When it sees an insect, it darts into the air. It especially likes bees, wasps, and ants. The bird grabs the insect in its mouth and returns to its perch. Then, it gives its prey a real thrashing.

Bees, wasps, and ants have stingers. They have *exoskeletons*. (An exoskeleton is outside a body. It covers it. People don't have exoskeletons. Their skeletons are *inside* their bodies.) The green bee-eater doesn't want to eat poison stingers or hard beaks. The green bee-eater thrashes its prey until these parts fall off. The beating also breaks the exoskeleton apart.

1. The green bee-eater breaks apart the exoskeleton of its prey so that
   - **a.** it can eat the soft insides.
   - **b.** it can find its poison stinger.
   - **c.** it can return to its perch.
   - **d.** it can dart into the air.

2. A *synonym* is a word that means the same thing as another word. A synonym for *beating* is
   - **a.** covering.
   - **b.** thrashing.
   - **c.** perching.
   - **d.** searching.

3. The green bee-eater can be found in parts of
   - **a.** Africa and North America.
   - **b.** Europe and Asia.
   - **c.** South America and Antarctica.
   - **d.** Asia and Africa.

4. From the story, you can tell that
   - **a.** no birds eat bees.
   - **b.** some birds eat bees.
   - **c.** some bees eat birds.
   - **d.** all birds eat bees.

5. When do you find out what is giving the bee a thrashing?
   - **a.** the title
   - **b.** the first paragraph
   - **c.** the second paragraph
   - **d.** the last paragraph

Name: ______________________________

Only Green

"Only green," Jack said. "I will only eat green foods. I will eat kiwis, peas, celery, and green apples. That's it. I've said it once, and I'll say it a thousand times more. I'm only going to eat green food."

Jack said it once, and he said it a thousand times more. He did what he said he would do. He only ate green food. Everyone tried to change Jack's mind, but Jack kept his resolution. If he had ice cream, it had to be lime. If he ate beans, they had to be lima beans.

Jack's father was angry. He yelled, "Eating only green food is not a good resolution! It is a bad resolution! You must eat many kinds of food. To grow and stay healthy, you need foods from every food group."

"I have a solution," Jack's brother Jerome said. Then, Jerome gave something to Jack. They were glasses with green lenses. Jack put them on. All kinds of food from every food group looked green when he was wearing his glasses. Now Jack could keep his resolution and still stay healthy!

1. What might Jack eat when he is not wearing his glasses?
   - **a.** cherries
   - **b.** pizza
   - **c.** hot dogs
   - **d.** lettuce

2. When you make a *resolution*,
   - **a.** you decide to do something and then change your mind.
   - **b.** you stop eating.
   - **c.** you decide to do something and stick to it.
   - **d.** you eat anything you want.

3. Why was Jack's father angry?
   - **a.** He was afraid that Jack was not making healthy choices.
   - **b.** He didn't want Jack to eat all the kiwis.
   - **c.** He thought that Jack was growing too fast.
   - **d.** He was tired of Jack yelling.

4. Most likely, if Jack had said he would only eat blue food,
   - **a.** Jerome would have given him glasses that had red lenses.
   - **b.** Jerome would have given him glasses that had purple lenses.
   - **c.** Jerome would have given him glasses that had pink lenses.
   - **d.** Jerome would have given him glasses that had blue lenses.

5. Another title for this story might be
   - **a.** "How to Grow Fast."
   - **b.** "A Green Resolution."
   - **c.** "The Best Things to Eat."
   - **d.** "Why Kiwis and Peas Are Healthy Foods."

Name: ____________________

Write On!

Think of something you learned about the color green from all the stories in this unit. Pick one or two things. Then, write a play in which you tell about:

- What you learned
- Where you learned it (fiction or nonfiction story)
- When you learned it (what part of the story)
- Why it was interesting
- Make sure your play has a title, a setting, and a cast.

Name: ______________________________

Tied Together

Two men are tethered together. They are tied together with a string that is just ten inches long. Why are the men's hands tied together?

At the age of three, David Brown lost one of his eyes from an illness. Soon, he lost the sight in his other eye, too. Some children would try to pick fights with Brown. They would call him "little blind boy." Brown did not let that get him down. He would say, "I bet I can beat you in a race."

Today, Brown is one of the fastest sprinters in the world. He has won many medals in the Paralympic Games and other races. Brown needs a sighted guide tethered to him when he runs. The guide makes sure Brown stays in his lane. The guide has to match Brown's stride and be just as fast.

1. Why might it be hard for Brown to find a guide?
   - a. No one wants to be tied together.
   - b. There are no sighted guides.
   - c. Most tethers are longer than ten inches.
   - d. Brown is faster than most people.
2. When a person is *tethered*, that person
   - a. is a runner. b. is tied. c. is blind. d. is fast.
3. From the story, you can tell that
   - a. Brown doesn't know how to run alone.
   - b. Brown has won ten medals.
   - c. Brown lost his sight when he was old.
   - d. in some races, runners run in their own lanes.
4. Most likely, if Brown lost a race,
   - a. he would stop running.
   - b. he would try to pick a fight.
   - c. he would not give up running.
   - d. he would say the race was not fair.

Name: ______________________________

The Fastest Runner

"Why don't you try harder?" Ron asked his friend Stephanie. "I know you can go faster." Stephanie just shrugged. She didn't like going at a fast pace. She liked to walk slowly and just amble along. Everyone teased Stephanie because she was so slow. Stephanie would just smile and say that she had no reason to run so fast.

One day, there was a race at the city park. Everyone at Stephanie's school had to enter the race. Everyone was sure that Stephanie would lose. When the race started, Stephanie was last. Then, Stephanie suddenly started to speed up. She overtook runner after runner and won the race.

"You didn't stroll. You didn't amble. You raced!" Ron said. "You are the fastest! Did you win so that people will stop teasing you?"

"No," Stephanie said, "I saw a snake."

1. A *synonym* is a word that means the same thing as another word. A synonym for *stroll* is
   a. race. **b.** enter. **c.** amble. **d.** tease.

2. Most likely, Stephanie didn't run fast before the race because
   a. she wanted to be teased.
   b. she didn't feel she had a reason to run fast.
   c. she wanted Ron to be her friend.
   d. she didn't want to be teased for being so slow.

3. From the story, you can tell that Stephanie
   a. does not like being close to snakes.
   b. can only run slower than the other students in her school.
   c. likes to stop and look at snakes.
   d. ran fast so people would stop teasing her.

4. Most likely, how did the people who had teased Stephanie before the race feel when she won?
   a. angry **b.** sad **c.** afraid **d.** surprised

Name: ______________________________

Live from the Racetrack!

"Good morning, boys and girls! Good morning, mammals, birds, reptiles, and insects! I'm here reporting live at the Woodland Racetrack. This is going to be an amazing race. The sidelines are crowded with spectators. All the spectators are looking at the starting line. The hare is ready. The turtle is ready. The bell goes off, and the contestants are off!

"The hare dashes ahead! He is far in the lead! The turtle has barely made headway. He is just plodding along, slow and steady. What's this? The turtle has stopped! He is giving up! The crowd is booing.

"What's this? The hare has stopped. He is going backward! He's run back to the turtle! Now, he's saying something to the turtle. The turtle has gotten up! He's moving again, slow and steady! The hare is right by his side, matching his stride! They cross the finish line together, and the crowd goes wild! All the spectators are throwing flowers and shouting, 'Hooray!'"

1. What do you know about the reporter?
   - **a.** The story is true, so it has to be an insect or a bird.
   - **b.** The story is fiction, so it has to be a mammal or a bird.
   - **c.** The story is true, so it has to be a boy or a girl.
   - **d.** The story is fiction, so it could be a boy, a girl, a mammal, a bird, a reptile, or an insect.

2. If a person is a *contestant*, that person
   - **a.** is a spectator.
   - **b.** is a boy or a girl.
   - **c.** is in a race or a contest.
   - **d.** is a reptile or an insect.

3. What happens first?
   - **a.** The hare matches the turtle's stride.
   - **b.** The hare dashes ahead.
   - **c.** The hare and the rabbit cross the finish line together.
   - **d.** The hare goes backward.

4. This story is mainly about
   - **a.** how the crowd goes wild.
   - **b.** a race in which one contestant helps another.
   - **c.** a reporter at the Woodland Racetrack.
   - **d.** what made the crowd boo.

Name: ______________________

An Extra Leg

Sarah Reinertsen was running. She was in a marathon. A marathon is a 26-mile-long race. A man was running next to Sarah. He was carrying something. It was an extra leg. Who was the man running next to Sarah? Why was he carrying an extra leg?

Sarah lost her leg when she was only seven years old. As Sarah said, she was "a one-legged girl in a two-legged world."

When she was 11, she saw a man sprinting in a race. The man had an artificial leg. Sarah was inspired by the man. She went home and started running.

Sarah got a coach. The coach helped her train. He ran with Sarah in the marathon. He carried an extra leg for her in case she needed it. Sarah finished that race. Then, she finished an even harder race. It was a triathlon. For that race, Sarah had to swim almost two and a half miles. Then, she had to bike 112 miles. After that, she had to run a marathon! She did it all without stopping.

1. When Sarah ran in the triathlon, she
   - **a.** had to carry an extra leg.
   - **b.** had to run farther than she swam.
   - **c.** had to swim farther than she biked.
   - **d.** had to run farther than she biked.

2. Who was the person carrying the extra leg?
   - **a.** a man running a triathlon
   - **b.** Sarah
   - **c.** a man who inspired Sarah
   - **d.** Sarah's coach

3. When you want to do something because you saw someone else do it first, you are
   - **a.** running.
   - **b.** sprinting.
   - **c.** inspired.
   - **d.** finished.

4. Most likely, what did Sarah mean when she said she was "a one-legged girl in a two-legged world"?
   - **a.** A person needs two legs to do many things in this world.
   - **b.** The world is standing on two legs.
   - **c.** Everyone in the world needs an extra leg.
   - **d.** Most people in the world only have one leg.

5. This story is mainly about
   - **a.** when Sarah lost her leg.
   - **b.** how far Sarah ran.
   - **c.** a runner who carried an extra leg.
   - **d.** a runner with an artificial leg.

Name: ______________________________

Shark Attack

Estrella said, "A shark attacked me yesterday."

When Oscar heard this, he was shocked. "How can you sound so calm?" he asked. "I'd still be shaking in fear." He thought for a moment, and then he said, "I know why you sound so calm. You escaped with no injuries. You weren't hurt at all."

"I escaped," Estrella said, "but I was only able to manage it because I lost an arm."

Now Oscar was really shocked. "That's horrible!" he cried. "Did it bleed a lot?"

"In a year, you won't be able to tell I was attacked," Estrella said. "And to answer your question, no. It didn't bleed at all."

"How is that possible?" Oscar asked. "How can you not bleed when you lose a limb?"

"I don't have any blood," Estrella said calmly. "No sea star does. We just pump seawater in and out of our bodies when we want to move. Like all sea stars, if I lose a limb, it will regenerate. That means a new one will grow back."

1. This story is fiction (made up), but it has facts in it. Which answer is a fact?
   - a. Sea stars do not have blood.
   - b. Sea stars live on dry land.
   - c. Sea stars can talk.
   - d. Sea stars do not have arms.

2. When an animal is *injured*, it is
   - a. hurt.
   - b. calm.
   - c. shocked.
   - d. attacked.

3. How does a sea star move?
   - a. by regenerating
   - b. by shaking all of its limbs
   - c. by pumping seawater in and out of its body
   - d. by being calm

4. When do you find out that Estrella is a sea star?
   - a. at the beginning so that you will be shocked
   - b. at the beginning so that you will forget about the shark
   - c. at the end so that you will know how to escape
   - d. at the end so that you will be surprised

5. Oscar won't be so shocked the next time Estrella tells him she lost an arm because now he knows that
   - a. sharks don't eat sea stars.
   - b. sea stars can swim away.
   - c. sea stars' limbs can regenerate.
   - d. sea stars have more than one limb.

Name: ______________________________

Write On!

Three of the stories in this unit are about human contestants. Choose one or two of the contestants from these stories. Then, write a live report about a race (like the story "Live from the Racetrack!") between them. In your report, tell where you are, who is racing, what happens, and who wins.

Name: ________________________________

Sky Fish

Christine Blamer was walking home. Suddenly, it started to rain. It wasn't raining water. It was raining fish! Hundreds of fish were falling from the sky. The fish were alive!

Blamer lived in Lajamanu. Lajamanu is in Australia. It is a tiny desert town. It is in the outback. It is far away from the ocean. There are not any lakes or rivers close by. How could it be raining fish?

Scientists say that the fish were picked up in a waterspout. A waterspout is like a small tornado that happens over water. The fish were carried high in the air. As one scientist said, "They were pretty much frozen." The people in town gathered up the fish. What did they eat for dinner that night? They feasted on fresh fish!

1. The story does not tell us
   - **a.** where the fish fell.
   - **b.** how the fish came to the town.
   - **c.** what day the fish fell.
   - **d.** what the people did to the fish.
2. Most likely, how did the people in Lajamanu feel?
   - **a.** shocked and lucky
   - **b.** shocked and mad
   - **c.** scared and lonely
   - **d.** scared and sad
3. How was it possible that the fish were still alive?
   - **a.** They had been cooked.
   - **b.** They found food in the sky.
   - **c.** They had only been partly frozen.
   - **d.** They fell into a lake.
4. This story is mainly about
   - **a.** fish falling from the sky.
   - **b.** a girl named Christine.
   - **c.** waterspouts.
   - **d.** what people can do with fish.

Name: ______________________

The Wager

Wind boasted that he was stronger than Sun. Sun said, "See that man over there with the sweater on? I'll wager you that you're not strong enough to remove that sweater from that man."

Wind said, "I'll take that bet! It will be easy because I can blow down enormous trees." Then, Wind took some deep breaths and began to blow. Wind blew so hard that the man almost fell down! Still, the man didn't take off his sweater. Instead, he buttoned it up, crossed his arms, and pressed them tightly to his chest.

When Wind admitted defeat, it was Sun's turn to try. Sun rose high in the sky. He burned fiercely, and the man began to swelter. With sweat dripping down his face, the man unbuttoned his sweater and took it off.

1. What might you want if you are *sweltering*?

- **a.** a cold drink
- **b.** a warm coat
- **c.** a hot dinner
- **d.** thick socks

2. Why did Wind think that he was stronger than Sun?

- **a.** He could take deep breaths.
- **b.** He could blow people down.
- **c.** He could blow down enormous trees.
- **d.** He could blow buttons off sweaters.

3. When a person makes a *wager*, that person

a. blows. **b.** buttons up. **c.** breathes. **d.** bets.

4. Most likely, the author wanted you to learn that

- **a.** if you blow down a big tree, you are the strongest.
- **b.** you can be strong in different ways.
- **c.** when you are strong, you never admit defeat.
- **d.** it is okay to boast if you are strong.

Name: ______________________________

Hurricane at Sea

August 15, 2017
Heading east from Boston Harbor

Dear Mom and Dad,

I'm about to sail through my first hurricane at sea! I thought we would head into port. I thought we would stay by land. We're not! The harbor is a dangerous place for big ships during hurricanes.

Ships are made with steel. They have hard sides. Docks are made with concrete pilings. When ships are tied up, the big waves make the ships smash against the concrete pilings over and over. The ships get damaged. Their sides get weakened. Sometimes, the big waves break a docked ship loose. When that happens, the ship is nothing more than a floating wrecking ball.

That's why we're headed out. Captain says not to worry because he's been tracking the hurricane. He's heading away from it so that we'll be out of its path.

Love,
Kenji

1. Why is the ship like "a floating wrecking ball" when it becomes loose?
   a. It is hard and can smash and crash into things.
   b. It can float safely in the water.
   c. Its steel sides are crushed into balls.
   d. It sinks when its sides are weakened.

2. When a ship captain finds out that a hurricane is coming, he or she will
   a. take the ship to a harbor and dock it.
   b. take the ship out to sea away from the hurricane.
   c. take the ship out to sea and into the hurricane.
   d. take the ship to a harbor and leave it untied.

3. From the story, you can tell that
   a. this is Kenji's first hurricane at sea.
   b. Kenji has sailed through a hurricane before.
   c. Kenji didn't know where they were headed.
   d. Kenji wanted the ship to stay in the harbor.

4. Most likely, the ship Kenji is on
   a. has weak sides.
   b. has damaged sides.
   c. has sides made of steel.
   d. has sides made of paper.

Name: ______________________________

Storm Danger

One minute, you are fine. The next minute, you see a wave. The wave is thousands of feet high! It is racing toward you at 25 miles per hour! You can't escape! The wave hits, and you are completely blinded. You can barely breathe. The wave covers you completely, but you are dry. There is not a drop of water for miles around. How can this be?

You are in a sandstorm. Hurricanes are storms with high winds that start at sea. Sandstorms are different. They have high winds, but they start over land. Often, they are in desert areas. The wind picks up sand. It picks up the top layer of dirt or soil. It lifts the soil into a huge wall, and then it blows it across the land.

Sandstorms have shut down airports. They have made all street traffic stop because no one could see. During one sandstorm, desert soil from Africa was lifted high into the sky. The sand blew across the Atlantic Ocean. It made the sunsets in Florida very red.

1. How are hurricanes different from sandstorms?
   - **a.** Hurricanes start over land.
   - **b.** Hurricanes start over water.
   - **c.** Hurricanes cause big waves.
   - **d.** Hurricanes do not have high winds.
2. From the story, you can tell that when there is a lot of sand and dirt in the sky,
   - **a.** there is a hurricane in the Atlantic Ocean.
   - **b.** airports have been shut down.
   - **c.** you will not be able to breathe for one minute.
   - **d.** it might make the sunset look very red.
3. Why might a sandstorm be bad for a farmer?
   - **a.** It helps his plants grow.
   - **b.** It blows good topsoil away.
   - **c.** It makes his farm too wet.
   - **d.** It blows the dirt off his airplane.
4. This story is mainly about
   - **a.** storms in Africa.
   - **b.** different kinds of waves.
   - **c.** why it is hard to breathe.
   - **d.** a kind of desert storm.
5. In the story, the wave is moving at
   - **a.** 25 miles per second.
   - **b.** 35 miles per second.
   - **c.** 25 miles per hour.
   - **d.** 35 miles per hour.

Name: ______________________________

Alex and Bonnie

Juan said, "Hannah, I want to tell you about Alex and Bonnie. They both died. Alex died in the Appalachian Mountains. Bonnie died at sea."

Hannah gasped. "Juan," she said, "that is horrible news. I'm so sorry. I'm sure you must feel very sad."

Juan asked, "Why is it horrible news? Why should I feel sad? It's good that they died. Everyone was happy. They were happiest with Bonnie's death."

Hannah was puzzled. She asked, "How can it be good that Alex and Bonnie died? Why was everyone happier with Bonnie's death?"

Juan said, "Every year, they pick new names for hurricanes. The names are alphabetical. They go boy, girl, boy, girl. There can be more than one hurricane happening at once. Naming them helps people keep track of the storms. The names help make sure that everyone gets the right information."

"Oh," Hannah said, laughing. "Now I understand. It was better for Bonnie to die at sea because that means she didn't make landfall. No cities were flooded. She did less damage."

1. If you only read the first part of the story,
   - **a.** you would know what Alex is.
   - **b.** you would know that Bonnie was sick.
   - **c.** you might have wanted to dance.
   - **d.** you might have felt upset.

2. The first two hurricanes of 2016 were named *Alex* and *Bonnie*. What were the third and fourth hurricanes named?
   - **a.** *Nicole* and *Otto*
   - **b.** *Lisa* and *Eric*
   - **c.** *Adam* and *Betty*
   - **d.** *Colin* and *Danielle*

3. What can you tell about Hurricane Alex from the story?
   - **a.** It did less damage than Bonnie.
   - **b.** It started after Bonnie.
   - **c.** It made landfall.
   - **d.** It was the second hurricane of the year.

4. You can sum up this story by saying it is about
   - **a.** how boys and girls are named.
   - **b.** why it is better to die at sea.
   - **c.** a boy telling a girl about hurricanes.
   - **d.** what storms cause the most damage.

5. When something is *damaged*, it is
   - **a.** helped.
   - **b.** hurt.
   - **c.** hungry.
   - **d.** hot.

Name: ______________________________

Write On!

Write a letter to someone you know. Begin your letter with the date and the city from where you are writing. Your letter can be about anything you want, but it must include at least four facts about hurricanes and strong winds. Use the information from the stories in Unit 8 to help you.

Name: ______________________________________

One of Seven

There are seven. Seven what? There are seven continents. A continent is a large landmass. One continent has the world's second-longest river. The river is not the longest, but it has the most water.

A snake lives on this continent. It is the heaviest snake in the world. Some weigh over 500 pounds! This snake can swim. Its nostrils and eyes are on top of its head. This allows it to breathe and see while it is partly underwater. This snake does not poison its prey. Instead, it squeezes, or constricts, it.

What river is it? What snake is it? What continent are they on? It is the Amazon River. It is the anaconda snake. Both are in South America.

1. A *continent*
   - **a.** is a river with lots of water in it.
   - **b.** is a heavy snake.
   - **c.** is a kind of poison.
   - **d.** is a large landmass.

2. Why wasn't the title of this story "South America"?
   - **a.** The author wanted you to think about what there could be seven of.
   - **b.** The author wanted you to learn the number seven.
   - **c.** The author didn't think the continent's name was important.
   - **d.** The author thought the river's name was more important.

3. If you *constrict* something, you
   - **a.** allow it. **b.** see it. **c.** squeeze it. **d.** breathe it.

4. Most likely, what will the author write about next?
   - **a.** a star
   - **b.** what she liked to eat
   - **c.** how to ride a bicycle
   - **d.** another continent

Name: ______________________________

Impossible House

Olive said, "I'm thinking of a house. It has four windows. There is one window on every side of the house. One window is on the east side. One window is on the west side. One window is on the north side. One window is on the south side. The windows are on every side, but they all face the same direction. Every window faces north."

At first, Olive's friend Tran thought that it couldn't be. He was about to say it was impossible. Then he thought of something. He smiled triumphantly. "I know where the house is!" he cried. "The house can only be on one continent. It has to be in Antarctica. The South Pole is in Antarctica. If the house is right on the South Pole, then every window will be facing north!"

1. This story is mainly about
   - **a.** a cold house.
   - **b.** a word puzzle.
   - **c.** a hot continent.
   - **d.** a dirty window.
2. When you smile *triumphantly*, you smile
   - **a.** angrily. **b.** proudly. **c.** sleepily. **d.** sadly.
3. What did Tran need to know before he could say where the house was?
   - **a.** what continent the South Pole was on
   - **b.** what continent you can build houses on
   - **c.** what continent is to the east
   - **d.** what continent most people live on
4. Who is Tran?
   - **a.** Olive's brother **b.** Olive's teacher **c.** Olive's friend **d.** Olive's uncle

Name: ____

Six or Seven?

Are there six continents, or are there seven? Australia is a continent. Africa is also a continent. Antarctica is one. North America is one. South America is one, too. What about Europe? What about Asia? Most people say that they are two continents. Others say that Europe and Asia make up a single continent. The continent is called Eurasia.

Asia is very different from Europe. They have very different cultures. They have very different histories. But they both share the same big landmass. Should they be one continent or two?

I do not think it has to be one or the other. I only think it's important to know why some people say six and why some people say seven. What is most important? Knowing where the continents are and which one you live on!

1. The author tells you her opinion in this story. How many continents does she think there are?

- **a.** There are six.
- **b.** There are seven.
- **c.** There can be six or seven.
- **d.** There can be six or seven plus the one you live on.

2. What continent is **always** counted as one?

a. Asia **b.** Europe **c.** Argentina **d.** Africa

3. In what part of the story are you told that Australia is a continent?

- **a.** paragraph 1
- **b.** paragraph 2
- **c.** paragraph 3
- **d.** paragraph 1 and 3

4. How many continents would there be if someone said the Americas were one continent?

- **a.** 5 if they counted Europe and Asia as Eurasia
- **b.** 4 if they counted Europe and Asia as Eurasia
- **c.** 3 if they counted Europe and Asia as Eurasia
- **d.** 2 if they counted Europe and Asia as Eurasia

Name: ______________________

Longest and Largest

Where is the world's longest river? It is on the same continent as an animal with a long lip. How long is the animal's lip? It is two feet long! This animal gives birth in the water. It eats grass. It can outrun a human.

Where is the world's largest hot desert? It is on the same continent as one of the world's largest reptiles. This reptile can go a long time without eating. How long can it survive without eating? It can go well over a year without eating! This reptile does not have lips. It can't seal its mouth. How does it keep from drowning when it is underwater? It has a flap in its throat. It can open and close the flap.

What river is the world's longest? What hot desert is the world's largest? What animal has a long lip? What reptile doesn't have a lip? The river is the Nile River. The desert is the Sahara. The animal is the hippopotamus. The reptile is the Nile crocodile. They are all in Africa.

1. What keeps a crocodile from drowning?
   - **a.** a flap in its throat
   - **b.** its lips
   - **c.** not breathing for a year
   - **d.** staying in the dry desert

2. When something is *sealed,*
   - **a.** it is shut tight.
   - **b.** it is left open.
   - **c.** it is in the water.
   - **d.** it is out of the water.

3. From the story, you can tell that
   - **a.** the Sahara is the biggest desert in the world.
   - **b.** some hot deserts are bigger than the Sahara.
   - **c.** all cold deserts are bigger than the Sahara.
   - **d.** a cold desert might be bigger than the Sahara.

4. This story is mainly about
   - **a.** continents.
   - **b.** some facts about Africa.
   - **c.** what lives in rivers.
   - **d.** how hot Africa is.

5. When something *survives,*
   - **a.** it can outrun a human.
   - **b.** it is the longest.
   - **c.** it can go without eating.
   - **d.** it is able to live.

Name: ______________________________

The Liar

"There's a new girl in my class," Pippa said. "None of us like her. She's a liar."

Pippa's mom said gently, "Are you sure, darling? Maybe she's just exaggerating. Maybe she's trying to make the truth more interesting or better because she thinks that then you will like her more."

"No," Pippa said, shaking her head. "She's not exaggerating. She's lying. She said she lived in Europe before moving to North America."

"That's quite possible," Pippa's mother said.

"She said she went to school in Asia! And she said she had two best friends. One friend lived in Asia. The other lived in Europe. She said they played together every day after school. That can't be true! She's a liar!"

"Ask her if she lived in Istanbul," Pippa's mother said.

"Why?" asked Pippa.

"Istanbul is a city in Turkey. It is unique. It is one of a kind. It is the only city in the world that straddles two continents. You can cross a bridge. Asia is on one side. Europe is on the other."

1. From the story, you can tell that Pippa lives in
   - a. Asia.
   - b. Europe.
   - c. South America.
   - d. North America.

2. If something is *one of a kind,* it
   - a. is very old.
   - b. is a lie.
   - c. is unique.
   - d. is exaggerated.

3. Is it possible that the new girl is telling the truth?
   - a. No, because she said her school was in Asia.
   - b. Yes, because she might have lived in Istanbul.
   - c. No, because she said her two friends played together.
   - d. Yes, because she might have lived in Africa when she was small.

4. How should Pippa feel when she learns that the new girl lived in Istanbul?
   - a. sorry for not believing her
   - b. mad at the girl for telling the truth
   - c. tired of the girl exaggerating
   - d. happy that none of the other girls like the new girl

5. Istanbul is a city in what country?
   - a. Tunisia
   - b. Tonga
   - c. Turkey
   - d. Tanzania

Name: ______________________________

Write On!

In the story "Six or Seven?" the writer gave two sides to an argument.

Imagine that there is an argument about what continent to travel to: South America or Africa. For each continent, write down why a person would want to visit and why a person would *not* want to visit. Then, tell which continent you would rather go to. Tell why you chose the one you did.

Use information from the stories "One of Seven" and "Longest and Largest" when you write your arguments.

Name: ______________________________

Not for Sale

You would pay 1 million dollars! You would pay 10 million dollars! You would pay 100 million dollars! It is never enough. You can never buy it. It will never be for sale. What is it?

It is a panda bear. All the panda bears in the world come from China. China is very proud of its pandas. China lends its pandas to zoos around the world. It lends them, but it does not sell them.

What is the origin of the panda-bear name? How did the name come about? No one is sure. Some people think it came from a native word that means "bamboo eater." Pandas do eat a lot of bamboo. In just one year, a panda might eat more than 10,000 pounds of bamboo!

1. If you see a panda in a zoo outside of China,
- **a.** you know that the zoo paid 1 million dollars for it.
- **b.** you know that the zoo paid 10 million dollars for it.
- **c.** you know that the zoo paid 100 million dollars for it.
- **d.** you know that the panda is being lent to the zoo.

2. If a zoo has a panda,
- **a.** the zoo must have a way of getting bamboo.
- **b.** the zoo must make people pay to get in.
- **c.** the zoo must be in China.
- **d.** the zoo must have black and brown bears, too.

3. The origin of the name *panda* may come from a native word that means
- **a.** "not for sale."
- **b.** "bamboo eater."
- **c.** "China."
- **d.** "never enough."

4. When someone is *proud*, they are
- **a.** very upset.
- **b.** very pleased.
- **c.** very angry.
- **d.** very rich.

Name: ____________________

The New Word

"I'm trying to make up a new word," Kelly said. "Languages change over time. Think about the phrase *couch potato*. A couch potato is a person who is being lazy. All that person does is sit on a couch and do nothing. That phrase was invented in the 1970s. I want to invent a new word today. I want people to start saying my new word, just like they started saying 'couch potato.'"

"Maybe you should think of a new word meaning 'there is a spider on your arm,'" Kelly's friend Melissa said.

"Why would I want to make up a word for that?" Kelly asked. "You know I hate spiders!"

"That's why you should know that there is one on your arm," Melissa said.

"AAAAAGH!" Kelly screamed.

"That's a great new word!" Melissa said.

1. Someone called a *couch potato* would most likely be
   - **a.** walking in the park.
   - **b.** eating at a friend's house.
   - **c.** watching TV all day.
   - **d.** playing soccer.
2. When was the phrase "couch potato" invented?
   - **a.** the 1960s **b.** the 1970s **c.** the 1980s **d.** the 1990s
3. One sentence that best sums up this story is:
   - **a.** A girl is trying to invent a new word.
   - **b.** A girl found out languages never change.
   - **c.** Two girls were afraid of spiders.
   - **d.** Two girls talked about potatoes while on the couch.
4. When did Kelly say she hated spiders?
   - **a.** after she screamed
   - **b.** before she said what she was trying to do
   - **c.** after she was told she made a great new word
   - **d.** before she was told there was one on her arm

Name: ____________________

Cinquain Poems

Cinquain poems are written like this:

Line 1: one word
Line 2: two words
Line 3: three words
Line 4: four words
Line 5: one word

Sometimes they are about a person, a place, or a thing and are written like this:

Line 1: one noun
Line 2: two adjectives
Line 3: three *-ing* words
Line 4: four-word phrase
Line 5: another word about the noun

Zoctopolly
Strange, wild
Traveling, exploring, floating
Dances over spinning planets
Welcome!

Books
Wonderful, exciting
Teaching, reading, laughing
Brings wild, crazy adventures
Read!

1. From the text, you can tell
   - **a.** a cinquain poem can only be written about exciting things.
   - **b.** a cinquain poem can be about anything you want.
   - **c.** a cinquain poem has to be about a noun.
   - **d.** a cinquain poem has to have seven lines.

2. Most likely, how does the author feel about reading?
   - **a.** She doesn't like it because there are so many pages.
   - **b.** She wants to be the only one who reads.
   - **c.** She likes it because she can learn exciting things.
   - **d.** She does not like adventure stories.

3. In what poem did the author write about a made-up thing?
   - **a.** "Welcome"
   - **b.** "Books"
   - **c.** "Cinquain"
   - **d.** "Zoctopolly"

4. Most likely, if the author met a Zoctopolly, how would she feel?
   - **a.** happy to meet it
   - **b.** unhappy because it looked strange
   - **c.** like slamming the door in its face
   - **d.** like hiding under a chair

Name: ____________________

Disaster

An earthquake strikes. Buildings collapse and fall down. People say, "It is a disaster." A big wave hits. Buildings are washed away. People say, "It is a disaster." Your mother sees your room. Nothing is put away. It is so messy that you can't even see the floor! Your mother says, "Your room is a disaster!"

A disaster is when something bad happens. The word *disaster* comes from two old Greek words. The Greek word *dis* means "bad." The Greek word *aster* means "star." How did these two Greek words come to mean that something bad happened?

Look up at the night sky. It is filled with stars and planets. The night sky does not always look the same. The stars and planets seem to move. Their position depends on the time of night and the time of year. If something bad happened, the Greeks used to blame the stars and planets. They said bad things happened when the stars and planets were in the wrong place!

1. When something *collapses,*
   - **a.** it falls.
   - **b.** it is messy.
   - **c.** it is in the wrong place.
   - **d.** it looks the same.
2. This story is mainly about
   - **a.** disasters around the world.
   - **b.** stars and planets.
   - **c.** why bad things happen.
   - **d.** how a word came about.
3. If something bad happened long ago, a Greek person might
   - **a.** blame it on the size of the planets.
   - **b.** blame it on seeing a black cat on a planet.
   - **c.** blame it on the position of the planets.
   - **d.** blame it on their mother.
4. Most likely, what could cause a disaster?
   - **a.** ice cream
   - **b.** seeing a good friend
   - **c.** a broken water pipe
   - **d.** putting on a seatbelt
5. From the story, you can tell that the night sky
   - **a.** always looks the same.
   - **b.** does not look the same in winter as it does in summer.
   - **c.** can never be looked at.
   - **d.** has more stars in the winter.

Name: ____________________________

When April Comes

At last, the rain had stopped! Ryan wanted to roller-skate in the park before it started to rain again. Ryan's friend Brian said, "No, we can't right now. We can do it when April comes."

Ryan said, "Since we're not going to go roller-skating, let's ride our bikes. We can ride around the block." Once again, Brian told him no. Brian said that it was better for them to wait until April arrives.

Ryan was frustrated. He was losing his patience. It had been raining cats and dogs! Finally, the rain had stopped, but it seemed as if Brian didn't want to go outside. Ryan said, "April is a week away! The forecast says it's going to rain again before the end of the month. We will lose our opportunity to play outside if we wait for April to come!"

There was a knock on the door. Brian opened it. A girl was standing there. "I'm April," she said to Ryan. "Brian told me you'd wait for me. Let's go outside before it starts to rain again."

1. From the story, you can tell that the word *April*
   - **a.** is always the name of a girl.
   - **b.** is always the name of a month.
   - **c.** can be the name of a month and a girl.
   - **d.** cannot be the name of a month and a girl.

2. From the story, you can tell that Ryan thought Brian
   - **a.** was waiting for his friend April.
   - **b.** was waiting for the month of April.
   - **c.** wanted to go outside and ride bikes.
   - **d.** wanted to go outside and roller-skate.

3. If you *no longer have the opportunity to do something,*
   - **a.** you can do it over and over.
   - **b.** you have to wait a week and a month.
   - **c.** you can go outside when it is raining.
   - **d.** you lose your chance to do it.

4. What was the weather forecast?
   - **a.** It was going to rain again before the end of the month.
   - **b.** It was going to rain again at the beginning of April.
   - **c.** It was going to stop raining after the end of the month.
   - **d.** It was going to stop raining on the first day of April.

5. When Ryan said it had been *raining cats and dogs*, he meant
   - **a.** cats and dogs had been falling from the sky.
   - **b.** there were a lot of pets outside.
   - **c.** it had been raining a lot.
   - **d.** he was frustrated with his pets.

Name: ______________________________

Write On!

Write a cinquain poem (see page 62) about one of the stories or characters in this unit. Next, write a second cinquain poem about a funny word—either one that you make up or one that you have heard before.

Name: ______________________________

The Tree Octopus

The tree octopus is in danger. It needs help. This endangered animal should be saved. It is the only octopus that can live on both land and water. It lives in rainforests. The air is moist in the rainforest. The octopus has special skin. The moist air and its skin keep the octopus from drying out.

Do you believe this? Do you think it is true? This story is not true. There is no tree octopus. It is a work of fiction. Octopuses cannot live on land. Many people believe it is real. They believe it because they read it on the Internet. A person made up the story. Then he made up more and more stories. He mixed fact and fiction. You shouldn't always believe what you read on the Internet.

1. If you only read the first paragraph of this story, you might think that
   - **a.** the tree octopus is real.
   - **b.** the tree octopus is made up.
   - **c.** the tree octopus is a mix of fact and fiction.
   - **d.** the tree octopus is like all other octopuses.
2. The author wrote this story so that you would know that everything you read on the Internet
   - **a.** has to be true.
   - **b.** is never true.
   - **c.** may not be true.
   - **d.** is a mix of fact and fiction.
3. Why does the author say that the octopus needs help?
   - **a.** It has special skin.
   - **b.** It can live on both land and water.
   - **c.** It lives in rainforests.
   - **d.** It is endangered.
4. If something is *moist*, it
   - **a.** is not muddy.
   - **b.** is not true.
   - **c.** is not dry.
   - **d.** is not special.

Name: ____________________

Seeing Through Walls

"I don't believe it," Lydia said. "I just don't believe it."

"He says it's true," Henry said. "Javier doesn't have a playful personality. He's a pretty serious boy. If he says that he can do it, then he probably can."

Lydia shook her head. "I'll believe it when I see it."

Lydia and Henry rode their bikes to Javier's house. When Javier opened the door, Lydia spoke. "What you're saying you can do is impossible. No one can look through a wall."

Javier took his two friends into the living room. He said, "I can look through a wall. Just watch!" Then, Javier went to the wall. He pulled open the curtains. Behind the curtains was a huge glass window. "This isn't the only wall I can look through!" Javier said.

1. An *antonym* is a word that means the opposite of another word. What word is an antonym for *playful*?
   - **a.** believable **b.** serious **c.** joyful **d.** impossible

2. What is the earliest moment in the story when you find out what Javier says he can do?
   - **a.** the first time Lydia speaks to Henry
   - **b.** the first time Lydia speaks to Javier
   - **c.** the second time Lydia speaks to Henry
   - **d.** the second time Lydia speaks to Javier

3. Most likely, if a wall has a window,
   - **a.** the window has curtains.
   - **b.** the window does not have curtains.
   - **c.** the wall can be looked through.
   - **d.** the wall cannot be looked through.

4. What sentence sums up this story?
   - **a.** A boy invents a way to look through walls.
   - **b.** Two friends are shown something impossible.
   - **c.** A boy plays a trick on his two friends.
   - **d.** Two friends look through a window.

Name: ______________________________

Eye Test

Look at the lines. Which line is longer? Put a check by it.

Look at the elephant. Write down how many legs you see.

Would you believe that the two lines above are the same length? And you know an elephant only has four legs, so what is going on? You are looking at optical illusions.

Optical illusions trick our brains. Our eyes see. They gather information. They send the information to our brain. Our brain takes it in. It processes it. It tries to make sense out of it. Colors and light can sometimes trick our brain. Patterns can sometimes trick our brains, too. Sometimes what our brain thinks it sees is not actually real!

1. An *optical illusion*
   - **a.** is your ears playing tricks on you.
   - **b.** is information about color.
   - **c.** is a kind of pattern.
   - **d.** is what our brain thinks it sees.

2. What does your brain do with information sent from your eyes?
   - **a.** It processes it.
   - **b.** It gathers it.
   - **c.** It tries to change it.
   - **d.** It makes sure it is real.

3. This story is mainly about
   - **a.** colors and light.
   - **b.** elephants.
   - **c.** optical illusions.
   - **d.** an eye test.

4. Which of the following is most likely an optical illusion?
   - **a.** water in a lake
   - **b.** water on a slide
   - **c.** water coming out of a hose
   - **d.** water flowing uphill

Name: ____________________

The TMW

On April 1, 1984, a news story came out. A new creature had been introduced to Florida. It came from Tasmania. The creature was known as the "Tasmanian Mock Walrus (TMW)." The TMW had whiskers. It was four inches long. It purred like a cat. It had four tiny paws. It had the personality of a hamster. It could be trained to use a litter box. Best of all, it ate cockroaches. Two pictures came with the report. One picture was of the TMW. The other photo was of people protesting.

What were the people protesting? The story said that the TMW might be banned. People could not have them as pets. Why not? Pest-control businesses did not want the TMW putting them out of business.

The story was a hoax. It was not true at all. The story came out on April Fool's Day. It was a hoax, but many people called wanting to know how they could get their own TMW. What did the TMW look like? It looked a lot like a naked mole rat!

1. What was said to be true about the TMW?
   - **a.** It purred like a walrus.
   - **b.** It had a soft tail.
   - **c.** It could be trained to use a litter box.
   - **d.** It came from Florida.

2. If something is a *hoax,* it is
   - **a.** introduced.
   - **b.** not introduced.
   - **c.** true.
   - **d.** not true.

3. From the story, you can tell that
   - **a.** no news is fake.
   - **b.** some news is fake.
   - **c.** most news is fake.
   - **d.** all news is fake.

4. The person who wrote the story most likely believed that
   - **a.** few people knew what a naked mole rat looked like.
   - **b.** no one wanted to get rid of cockroaches.
   - **c.** animals from other countries should be banned.
   - **d.** April is the best month to buy a pet.

5. This story is mainly about
   - **a.** a trick played on April Fool's Day.
   - **b.** a new creature.
   - **c.** why people were protesting.
   - **d.** cockroaches and pest-control businesses.

Name: ______________________________

Fake News

Ms. Veracity said, "Not all news is true. Sometimes, people make up news. They make up facts to trick people or to get what they want. Then there is news that is stranger than fiction. The news is true, but it is hard to believe. I am going to tell you two news items. One is true. The other is false. Listen and decide which one is not true.

"A man rode his horse to town on Friday. He stayed in town for four days and three nights. He left on Friday.

"A woman was digging in her backyard. She dug all the way to the other side of Earth and came out in China."

The students in Ms. Veracity's class looked at each other. Neither story sounded as if it could be true. The students were absolutely positive that no one could dig through the planet, but how could someone arrive on Friday and then leave on Friday only a few days later? Then Kareem said, "What if the horse's name was Friday?"

1. A *fact* is
   - **a.** something that is never true.
   - **b.** something that is sometimes true.
   - **c.** something that is the same as fiction.
   - **d.** something that is always true.

2. If the man arrived in town on a Monday, on what day did he leave?
   - **a.** Monday
   - **b.** Thursday
   - **c.** Friday
   - **d.** Saturday

3. What lesson did Ms. Veracity want her students to learn?
   - **a.** Always believe what you read.
   - **b.** Facts in news stories should be checked.
   - **c.** *Strange* and *fiction* are the same thing.
   - **d.** Digging holes can be dangerous.

4. What statement is absolutely, positively fiction?
   - **a.** Lions have cubs.
   - **b.** Cats have puppies.
   - **c.** Deer have fawns.
   - **d.** Cows have calves.

5. The phrase "stranger than fiction" means
   - **a.** it is stranger than something you could make up.
   - **b.** it is very strange, and it is made up.
   - **c.** strangers make up news items all the time.
   - **d.** it is always easy to spot the truth.

Name: ______________________________

Write On!

Explain what the phrase "stranger than fiction" means. Pick one example from the stories you read in this unit.

Next, write a story about a strange event or animal. Your story can be fact, fiction, or a mix of fact and fiction.

Have a friend read your story. See if they can pick out what is fact and what is fiction.

Name: ______________________________

Fortune Cookies

How did fortune cookies come about? The first ones were made long ago. They were made in the 1800s. They were made in Japan. They were made by hand. In 1914, an American man from Japan had opened a café. He started serving fortune cookies as a snack. They were a hit! Everyone loved them. Today, they are served in many places.

The cookies are hard. How are the fortunes put inside? The batter is put in a little cup. A metal plate keeps it flat. It is baked for only a few minutes. The dough is a warm, floppy circle. A fortune is put inside. Then, the dough is folded. The dough hardens as it cools. Today, most fortune cookies are made by machines.

1. When the story says, "They were a hit!" it means
   - a. that no one liked the cookies.
   - b. that everyone liked the cookies.
   - c. that the cookies were hit with a bat.
   - d. that the cookies were a snack.
2. When were fortune cookies first served in America?
   - a. 1800
   - b. 1814
   - c. 1900
   - d. 1914
3. How are most fortune cookies that are made today different from those that were made long ago?
   - a. Today, they are made by hand.
   - b. Today, they are made by machine.
   - c. Today, they have paper fortunes inside.
   - d. Today, they harden as they cool.
4. Most likely, if you cooked fortune-cookie batter for 30 minutes, the dough would
   - a. taste better.
   - b. be soft, floppy, and easy to fold.
   - c. taste like paper.
   - d. be too hard and burnt to fold.

Name: ______________________________

Dana's Invention

Dana said, "Don't drink that! It's my newest invention. I haven't tested it yet."

"How are you going to test it?" Ming asked curiously.

"I'll let Prince taste it," Dana said, putting a few drops on the palm of her hand and extending it out to her dog. Prince sniffed Dana's hand. Then he began to eagerly lick it. Prince's tail wagged wildly, so Dana decided to offer Prince some more.

As Prince eagerly lapped up more, a funny thing happened. Prince began to fade! Soon, he was invisible! The only thing that could be seen was his red collar!

Dana and Ming looked at each other. "Wow," Ming whispered. "Do you think we will ever see your dog again?"

"As soon as I invent something else . . ." Dana said.

1. If you *extend* something, you
   - **a.** cannot see it.
   - **b.** make it fade.
   - **c.** make it longer.
   - **d.** turn invisible.

2. How do you know Prince liked the taste of Dana's invention?
   - **a.** He stopped wagging his tail.
   - **b.** He eagerly lapped it up.
   - **c.** He sniffed Dana's hand.
   - **d.** He turned invisible.

3. This story can be summed up as
   - **a.** a true story about two friends and an invisible dog.
   - **b.** a fiction story about a girl who turns invisible.
   - **c.** a true story about a dog with an invisible collar.
   - **d.** a fiction story about a girl who makes her dog invisible.

4. What will the author probably write about next?
   - **a.** Dana's next invention
   - **b.** how Dana turns the blue collar red
   - **c.** how Dana and Ming ride bikes
   - **d.** what Dana and Ming eat for dinner

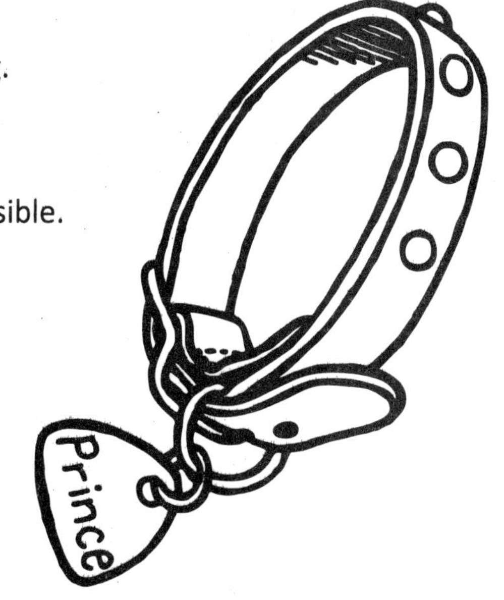

Name: ______________________________

100 Years Diary

January 1, 1900

Dear Diary,

I can't believe it is the start of a new century! I wonder what it will bring. I'm writing at night. My light comes from a lightbulb! No more writing by candlelight! There is nothing left for humans to invent.

January 1, 2000

Dear Diary,

As I write this, I can't help but think about how much things are changing. We have computers now. People communicate by sending emails. We have cell phones. We have fast cars and even faster planes. We send people into outer space! There is nothing left for humans to invent.

January 1, 2100

Dear Diary,

I'm glad it is a new century. I like living in space. We have everything we need here. Nothing new needs to be invented.

1. What diary entries are in the past?
   - a. Jan. 1, 2000
   - b. Jan. 1, 1900 and Jan. 1, 2000
   - c. Jan. 1, 1900 and Jan. 1, 2100
   - d. Jan. 1, 1900, Jan. 1, 2000, and Jan. 1, 2100
2. When people write or call each other, they are
   - a. inventing.
   - b. hiding.
   - c. growing.
   - d. communicating.
3. Most likely, the author thinks that
   - a. more things will be invented.
   - b. people should write by candlelight.
   - c. things have not changed over time.
   - d. people should not live in space.
4. From the story, you can tell that a *century* is
   - a. 1 year.
   - b. 10 years.
   - c. 100 years.
   - d. 1,000 years.

Name: ______________________________

Buttons

The buttons didn't line up. They didn't hold anything together, yet people still wore them. Why would people wear buttons that didn't line up? Why would they wear them if they didn't hold anything together?

Long ago, people had pins. They used the pins to hold their clothes together. Buttons were for something else. They were only for decoration. If you were rich, your buttons cost a lot. They might be gold. They might be silver. They might be painted. Some had pictures of people on them. Others had landscapes painted on them. Poor people didn't have fancy buttons. Their buttons were made of plain cloth or thread.

In the 1700s, something changed. Buttons could be made for less money. They could be made in factories. Some were cut from huge sheets of metal. Others were made from animal horns or shells. Buttons were so cheap that people started using them in a new way. They weren't just used for decoration anymore. People made buttonholes, and then they used the buttons to hold things up or together!

1. Why didn't people make buttonholes long ago?
   - **a.** Buttonholes cost too much to make.
   - **b.** People didn't have any thread.
   - **c.** It was hard to paint a buttonhole.
   - **d.** Buttons were only used for decoration.

2. This story is mainly about
   - **a.** rich people's buttons.
   - **b.** using pins long ago.
   - **c.** decorative and useful buttons.
   - **d.** cutting buttons from metal sheets.

3. A button with a *landscape* painted on it would most likely have
   - **a.** a picture of a mountain and trees.
   - **b.** a picture of a lady and her baby.
   - **c.** a picture of a king on a horse.
   - **d.** a picture of a lady sitting in a chair.

4. Why did people start using buttons in a new way?
   - **a.** People didn't want to decorate their clothes.
   - **b.** Buttons could be made cheaply.
   - **c.** People got tired of gold buttons.
   - **d.** People ran out of shells and animal horns.

5. When you *decorate* something, you
   - **a.** must paint it.
   - **b.** cut it from a metal sheet.
   - **c.** add something to make it prettier.
   - **d.** use it in a new way.

Name: ______________________________

Ali's Invention

It was time to go to lunch. Everyone raced down the hall and tried to get there first. Everyone crowded around the serving table. They pushed and shoved, all trying to get their food. Students carrying trays got knocked down. Someone spilled milk on Ali's shoes.

At recess, everyone wanted to go down the slide. Everyone pushed and shoved as they tried to get to the ladder. Ali got knocked in the side by someone's elbow. Ali gave up. Shaking his head, he walked away and sat on a bench. He didn't like the way things were. He wanted things to change.

Recess ended when the whistle blew. All the students raced to the door. They started pushing and shoving as they tried to get back to class. That's when Ali shouted. He bellowed so loud that everyone stopped. Everyone turned to stare at Ali. "I've invented something," Ali said. "My invention will stop all this pushing and shoving. It will improve life. It will make life better. It's called a 'line'!"

1. This story is mainly about
   - **a.** a boy who wanted to improve life.
   - **b.** why milk spilled on Ali's shoes.
   - **c.** a boy who pushed and shoved at recess.
   - **d.** how inventions have changed people.

2. What happened first?
   - **a.** Students raced down the hall.
   - **b.** Ali wanted things to change.
   - **c.** Someone spilled milk on Ali.
   - **d.** Ali sat on a bench.

3. Why didn't Ali go down the slide?
   - **a.** He hurt his elbow.
   - **b.** He wanted to sit on a bench first.
   - **c.** He gave up when he was knocked in the side.
   - **d.** He was still in line when recess ended.

4. When you *bellow*, you
   - **a.** sit on a bench.
   - **b.** push and shove.
   - **c.** want things to be better.
   - **d.** yell really loudly.

5. What is Ali hoping his invention will do?
   - **a.** stop students from getting to class
   - **b.** make it easier to get and do things
   - **c.** improve his chances of being first
   - **d.** help to keep things the way they are

Name: ____________________

Write On!

What do all of the stories in this unit have in common? Compare and contrast two of the stories from Unit 12. How are they similar? How are they different? What message did you learn from all of the stories?

Name: ____________________________

Only Twelve

There have been only twelve. It is not certain if there will ever be more. What have there been only a dozen of? There have only been twelve men who have walked on the moon. The first astronaut walked on the moon in 1969. The last astronaut walked on the moon in 1972.

The men are gone, but things have been left. Landing gear and moon buggies have been left. Flags and two golf balls have been left. All those things were brought to the moon, but astronauts left something else. The astronauts did not bring these things from Earth, but they left them. What are they?

They are footprints. The footprints will stay forever. They will not erode. There is no wind to blow and erase them. There is no water to wash them away.

1. A better title for this story might be
   - a. "Playing Golf on the Moon."
   - b. "What the Dozen Left."
   - c. "Astronauts."
   - d. "A Flag Forever."

2. When something *erodes*, it
   - a. stays forever.
   - b. washes or blows away.
   - c. is brought somewhere.
   - d. is left somewhere.

3. A man walked on the moon in
   - a. 1962.
   - b. 1976.
   - c. 1969.
   - d. 1973.

4. Most likely, landing gear was left on the moon because
   - a. it was not needed on the return trip.
   - b. astronauts knew the wind would blow it away.
   - c. it was needed to hang the flags on.
   - d. moving it would mess up the footprints.

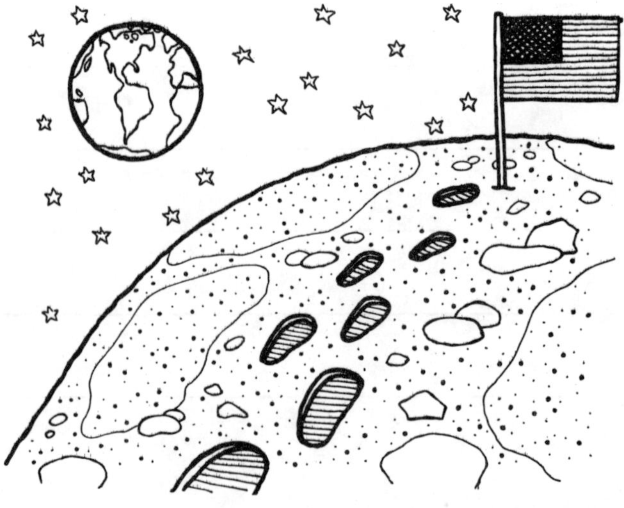

Name: ______________________

Why She Wept

"She's sobbing! She's weeping! She won't stop wailing! What's wrong?" An elderly couple had heard Damon's little sister's cries. They had come to investigate.

"Oh, don't worry about her," Damon reassured them. "She's just upset because our house was ruined."

"That's terrible!" the old lady said. "I'd be weeping and wailing, too, if my house were ruined."

"I warned her," Damon said. "I told her it would happen."

The old man and the old woman looked at each other. They wanted to help the poor girl who had lost her house. Before they could say anything, Damon spoke.

"Please excuse me," he said. "I'm going to take my sister back down to the beach so that we can build another house."

1. From the story, you can infer that the house was made of
   - **a.** rock.
   - **b.** wood.
   - **c.** sand.
   - **d.** stone.
2. When you *investigate,* you try
   - **a.** to find out why something happened.
   - **b.** to help someone.
   - **c.** to make someone feel better.
   - **d.** to warn someone.
3. Most likely, the elderly couple didn't know what the ruined house was made of because Damon
   - **a.** was wailing so much.
   - **b.** was reassuring his sister.
   - **c.** was telling them not to worry.
   - **d.** was not at the beach.
4. A *synonym* is a word that means the same thing as another word. What word is a synonym for *elderly*?
   - **a.** old
   - **b.** terrible
   - **c.** poor
   - **d.** little

Name: ______________________________

A Piece of Space

Kate wanted to hold a piece of outer space. Kate was not an astronaut. She didn't get into a spacesuit. She didn't get into a rocket. Still, Kate found an object from space that she could study. No one had ever seen it before. No one had ever touched it before.

Space is very far away. Our closest planet, Mars, is over 100 million miles from Earth! How could Kate hold a piece of outer space?

Kate put on a snowsuit. She got on a snowmobile. She rode over fields of ice in Antarctica. She looked for black spots. Meteorites fall to Earth all the time. They get buried in ice. Over time, the ice moves. Top layers erode. Bottom layers are pushed up. The buried meteorites rise to the surface. Their black color makes them easy to spot.

1. Why didn't Kate travel into space?
   - a. She didn't want to wear a spacesuit.
   - b. She wanted to ride a snowmobile.
   - c. She didn't want to ride in a rocket.
   - d. Space was too far away.
2. From the story, you can tell that
   - a. no meteorites fall to Earth.
   - b. all meteorites fall to Earth.
   - c. some meteorites fall to Earth.
   - d. most meteorites fall to Earth.
3. What makes the meteorites easy to spot?
   - a. The fields of ice are old.
   - b. The fields of ice are cold.
   - c. The fields of ice are white.
   - d. The fields of ice are thick.
4. Most likely, Kate studies
   - a. how to build snowmobiles.
   - b. how planets are formed.
   - c. what animals live in Antarctica.
   - d. how ice is eroded.

Name: ______________________________

Dinosaurs and Erosion

What is erosion? What does it have to do with dinosaurs? Erosion is when land is worn away by different forces. Water can wear land away. Wind can wear land away. Ice can wear land away, too. Erosion can change the shape of the coastline. It can make valleys. It can change the face of mountains. Erosion washes away sand. It moves dirt. It wears down rocks. A river helped make the Grand Canyon!

Dinosaurs lived long ago. Some of the dinosaurs were turned into fossils. When these dinosaurs died, they were quickly buried. Perhaps they sank in the mud. Perhaps a sandstorm buried them in sand. Over time, they were covered by more dirt. Many years later, they turned into stone.

What do dinosaurs have to do with erosion? Scientists go to places with lots of erosion. They can see layers of rock. They look for fossils in the rock. Sue is a big *Tyrannosaurus rex*. How was she found? A lady named Sue looked up at an eroding cliff. She saw Sue's bones sticking out!

1. Most likely, the dinosaur named Sue
   - **a.** did not live long ago.
   - **b.** is not a fossil.
   - **c.** is named after the person who found her.
   - **d.** was found in the Grand Canyon.

2. In order for a dinosaur fossil to form, the dinosaur
   - **a.** had to be eroded.
   - **b.** had to sink into mud.
   - **c.** had to be buried by a sandstorm.
   - **d.** had to be quickly buried.

3. Most likely, erosion can
   - **a.** wash away part of your school playground.
   - **b.** make you eat more ice cream.
   - **c.** help keep your room clean.
   - **d.** make the stars look brighter at night.

4. Erosion can be caused by what forces?
   - **a.** only water
   - **b.** water and ice
   - **c.** wind and water
   - **d.** water, wind, and ice

5. This story is mainly about
   - **a.** how a *Tyrannosaurus rex* was named.
   - **b.** how some fossils are found because of erosion.
   - **c.** how to make a fossil.
   - **d.** how dinosaurs lived long ago.

Name: ______________________________

Missing!

"He's missing!" Ethan wailed to his big sister Suzanna. "I've been playing with him all week. I don't know where he's gone. Please, Suzanna, help me find him. The sun is out, and I want to play with him."

Suzanna said gently, "Are you sure you didn't insult him? Did you say something to offend him? Perhaps you said something that hurt his feelings."

"No," Ethan said firmly. "I was never mean. I didn't do anything to insult or offend him. I even gave him my hat and scarf."

"Well, that was nice of you," Suzanna said.

"But he forgot to take them!" Ethan said, starting to wail again.

Suzanna said, "Let's get your scarf and hat. Then we can look for your friend." When Suzanna went outside with Ethan, she said, "Oh, it's nice and hot today!" Then she saw the scarf and hat. They were wet and soggy. That's when Suzanna knew where Ethan's friend was. "Ethan," she said, "Don't cry about your friend. Next time it snows, I will make you an even bigger snowman."

1. What does Ethan say in the first paragraph that gives you a hint about who Ethan's friend is?
   - **a.** "He's missing."
   - **b.** "I don't know where he's gone."
   - **c.** "Help me find him."
   - **d.** "The sun is out."

2. When something is *soggy*, it is
   - **a.** lost.
   - **b.** mean.
   - **c.** wet.
   - **d.** hurt.

3. From the story, you can tell that Ethan's friend
   - **a.** had melted.
   - **b.** was offended.
   - **c.** was insulted.
   - **d.** thought Ethan had been mean.

4. This story is mainly about
   - **a.** why you should not be mean.
   - **b.** a sister being kind to her brother.
   - **c.** a missing scarf and hat.
   - **d.** what happens when it is cold.

5. What did Suzanna think about Ethan's friend at first?
   - **a.** He should have taken better care of the hat.
   - **b.** He should have taken better care of the scarf.
   - **c.** He might have run away when he heard Ethan wailing.
   - **d.** He might have gone because Ethan said something mean.

Name: ______________________________

Write On!

Using the stories from Unit 13 to help you, explain what erosion is and what effect it has on Earth. Provide examples from the stories in Unit 13 that show how erosion can cause both small and very large changes to our planet.

Name: ____________________________

What Am I?

I only have two legs, but for 30 minutes I can run faster than a horse. I have feathers even though I can't fly. Have you guessed that I'm a bird?

What kind of bird am I? I'm the only bird in the world that has two toes. I have a really hard tread on my larger toe. The hard tread is like the thick sole of a boot. It protects my foot as I run.

I win all the avian records when it comes to tallest body, biggest eyes, and largest eggs. When my chicks hatch, they are the largest chicks in the world. They can be as big as grown chickens! Have you figured out yet what kind of avian creature I am? I am an ostrich!

1. What type of creature is a bird?
   a. a fish
   b. a mammal
   c. an avian
   d. an insect

2. This story is mainly about
   a. running.
   b. avian records.
   c. ostriches.
   d. toes.

3. Why does an ostrich have a hard tread on its larger toe?
   a. because it only has two toes
   b. to protect its foot
   c. because it is the tallest bird
   d. to help it protect its chicks

4. Most likely, the ostrich
   a. has long legs and little wings.
   b. can only fly over water.
   c. has short legs and big wings.
   d. can only fly when it is hot.

Name: ____________________

The Best Job

I have a very important job. I'm a shepherd. I am responsible for a flock of sheep. I keep my flock safe. I keep my flock together. I do not let any sheep stray. If a sheep begins to wander off, I run to it. I keep it from straying.

I needed training for my job, but the training was easy. It came naturally. That's because I tend to run around in circles. It helps, too, that I am fast. I run circles around my flock. As I run, I watch out for predators. No lion or leopard is going to eat one of my sheep while I'm on duty!

Most people think only dogs are trained to protect sheep. I'm an ostrich, and I can protect sheep, too!

1. When something *strays*,
   - **a.** it is trained.
   - **b.** it tends to run in circles.
   - **c.** it is on duty.
   - **d.** it wanders off.
2. Who is the "I" in this story?
   - **a.** an ostrich
   - **b.** a dog
   - **c.** a sheep
   - **d.** a leopard
3. What can you tell about ostriches from reading the story?
   - **a.** They can't be trained.
   - **b.** They tend to run in circles.
   - **c.** They eat insects and seeds.
   - **d.** They like to eat lions.
4. Think about where lions and leopards live. Most likely, what is another predator the ostrich will help protect his flock from?
   - **a.** a shark
   - **b.** a rabbit
   - **c.** a cheetah
   - **d.** a bear

Name: ______________________________

Fact or Fiction?

Sometimes, it is hard to tell the difference between fact and fiction. Read the following sentences. Do they sound like fact or fiction to you?

An ostrich eats a watch. An ostrich eats diamonds.

Ostriches have eaten watches and diamonds before. It is normal for ostriches to eat stones and other shiny things. This is because ostriches do not have teeth. They eat stones to help grind their food. The stones and hard, shiny things are not digested. Instead, they sit in the ostrich's gizzard. The gizzard is like a second stomach.

An ostrich is scared. It feels threatened. It hides its head in the sand.

Ostriches do not put their heads in the sand when they feel scared or threatened. It only looks that way. The ostrich has a small head. It has a big body. It has a long neck. When it bends down, its head looks as though it is buried because it is so hard to see. Ostriches can also run fast. They have strong legs. If they feel threatened, they will run away or kick.

1. Is it fact or fiction that an ostrich ate a diamond and digested it?
   - **a.** Fiction that it ate it, fact that it digested it.
   - **b.** Fiction that it ate it, fiction that it digested it.
   - **c.** Fact that it ate it, fiction that it digested it.
   - **d.** Fact that it ate it, fact that it digested it.

2. Why do ostriches eat stones?
   - **a.** The stones are needed to help grind up their food.
   - **b.** The stones help keep an ostrich's teeth sharp.
   - **c.** The stones are used when an ostrich feels threatened.
   - **d.** The stones help food go down their long necks.

3. Most likely, if an ostrich feels its chick is threatened, it will
   - **a.** kick at whatever is threatening its chick.
   - **b.** put its head in the sand.
   - **c.** bend down and hit it with its long neck.
   - **d.** run to a pile of stones and hide.

4. This story is mainly about
   - **a.** animals that have gizzards.
   - **b.** what will scare an ostrich.
   - **c.** some ostrich facts.
   - **d.** where a person can find diamonds.

Name: ______________________________

Planning Ahead

Long ago, the San people wandered across parts of South Africa. They ate berries and roots. They used bows and arrows to hunt animals. Sometimes, the climate was very dry. When it didn't rain for months, all the water holes would dry up. What did the San people do for water? How did they survive?

The San people had planned ahead. Earlier, they had found clutches of ostrich eggs. They had taken some of the eggs from the nests. (They were always careful to leave at least one egg in each nest. That was so there would always be more ostriches.) Then, the San made small holes in the ends of the eggs so that they could eat the insides.

The San would not throw away the empty eggshells. Instead, they turned them into water bottles! Once the shells were filled with water, the San would seal up the holes they had made. They would bury the eggs in the ground. The San would dig up the eggs when they needed water.

1. You can tell from the story that most likely

a. ostrich eggs have strong, thick shells.

b. ostrich eggs have thin, easy-to-break shells.

c. ostrich eggs taste better than berries and roots.

d. ostrich eggs not do not taste as good as berries and roots.

2. This story is mainly about

a. South Africa.

b. how the San used ostrich eggs.

c. water bottles.

d. living day to day.

3. Why did the San always leave at least one egg in each clutch?

a. so they could eat it later

b. so they could bury it later

c. so they could save it for when it rained

d. so at least one ostrich could hatch

4. If people *last* and *stay alive*, they

a. hunt. **b.** survive. **c.** wander. **d.** dig.

5. Most likely, what did the San seal the eggs with?

a. grass **b.** cement **c.** shoe polish **d.** glass

Name: ________________________________

A San Story

Long ago, the San people ate just like the leopard and the lion. They had to eat their food raw. They had no fire to brighten the long, dark nights.

One day, Mantis noticed that Ostrich's food smelled different. It smelled good. Mantis secretly watched Ostrich. He saw Ostrich take some fire from beneath his wing. Ostrich dipped his food in it. Then, Ostrich tucked the fire back under his wing.

Mantis knew that Ostrich would not give him fire. Mantis made a plan. "Come!" he said to Ostrich. "I found a tree that has delicious yellow plums on it." Ostrich came running. He immediately began to eat the low plums. "Higher! Higher! The most delicious plums are higher!" Mantis said. Ostrich began to eat the higher plums. He had to stretch out his wings in order to balance himself. That's when Mantis grabbed some fire.

Mantis gave the fire to the San. How did Ostrich feel? Ostrich was ashamed. Since then, he has never again used his wings to fly. He keeps them pressed against his sides to keep the little fire he has left.

1. If food is *raw*, it

a. is cooked. **b.** is not cooked. **c.** is delicious. **d.** is not delicious.

2. The San story explains

a. why ostriches don't like lions.
b. why ostriches can stretch so tall.
c. why ostriches are able to run so fast.
d. why ostriches can't fly.

3. Most likely, why was Ostrich ashamed?

a. He knew he should have shared the fire.
b. He ate all the plums on the tree.
c. He secretly watched Mantis eat.
d. He knew that his food smelled different.

4. Why did Mantis have to make a plan?

a. He was afraid to ask Ostrich for fire.
b. He wanted some of Ostrich's food.
c. He didn't want the San to have fire.
d. He knew Ostrich would not give him fire.

5. When did Mantis grab the fire?

a. before he made his plan
b. before he secretly watched Ostrich
c. after Ostrich tried to balance
d. after Ostrich was ashamed

Name: ______________________________

Write On!

Explain how the San planned ahead. How did this help them survive?

Next, explain how you would plan ahead if you learned you would be getting an ostrich for a pet. How would you need to plan ahead to make sure the ostrich was safe? How would you keep all your belongings safe? Most importantly, how would you plan ahead to make sure that *you* are kept safe? Use the information from Unit 14 to help you to write your response.

Name: ______________________________

What Did You Say?

In a restaurant, you ask for chips. You are not given potato chips. You are given french fries. Did you make a mistake? Did the person who gave you the french fries make a mistake? What is going on?

In England, people speak English. In the United States, people speak English, too. The two countries are far apart. They are separated by the Atlantic Ocean. Over time, languages change. Words may get new or different meanings.

In England, chips are french fries. If you want potato chips, you have to ask for crisps. In England, the trunk of your car is called the boot. A sweater is called a jumper. A cookie or a cracker is called a biscuit. Sneakers are trainers. The ground floor is the first floor. The first floor is the second floor!

1. If someone says, "Put the groceries in the boot," that person most likely lives in
   - **a.** the United States.
   - **b.** Uruguay.
   - **c.** England.
   - **d.** Egypt.

2. If you order chips at a restaurant in England, they will most likely bring you
   - **a.** tortilla chips.
   - **b.** french fries.
   - **c.** crackers.
   - **d.** biscuits.

3. From the story, you can tell that
   - **a.** languages never change.
   - **b.** only English words change.
   - **c.** sometimes, words may get new meanings over time.
   - **d.** English is only spoken in two countries.

4. What ocean separates England from the United States?
   - **a.** the Arctic
   - **b.** the Pacific
   - **c.** the Atlantic
   - **d.** the Indian

Name: ____________________

Something's Missing

Mark and Lucy read what was on the board. Then they looked at each other. Why would their teacher, Ms. Vowel, write what she did? Once again, Mark and Lucy read what was on the board.

This is an unusual paragraph. I'm curious how quickly you can find out what is so unusual about it. It looks so plain—you would think nothing was wrong with it. In fact, nothing is wrong with it! It is unusual, though. Study it. Think about it. You still may not find anything odd. If you work at it a bit, you might find out what is odd.

Then, Mark and Lucy knew! It was missing the most common letter in the English language!

1. From the story, you can tell that the most common letter in the English language is
   - **a.** *a*
   - **b.** *e*
   - **c.** *i*
   - **d.** *o*
2. A *synonym* is a word that means the same thing as another word. A synonym for *odd* is
   - **a.** plain.
   - **b.** wrong.
   - **c.** quick.
   - **d.** unusual.
3. What hint does the author give you about the answer to the teacher's question?
   - **a.** She tells you that you will like what you read.
   - **b.** She tells you that the teacher's name is Ms. Vowel.
   - **c.** She tells you that Lucy and Mark look at each other.
   - **d.** She tells you that something was on the board.
4. This story is mainly about
   - **a.** Mark and Lucy's reading lesson.
   - **b.** letters in the alphabet.
   - **c.** the most unusual letter in the English language.
   - **d.** some sentences without the letter *o*.

Name: ____________________

Riddles

An archaeologist studies the past. He or she digs up old buildings. They try to learn how people lived long ago. Riddles are not just from the present. Riddles are from the past, too. Archaeologists have dug up old walls and stones. They have found riddles etched or carved into the walls and stones!

Some examples of riddles from long ago are:

What loses its head every morning but gets it back every night?

I'm as light as a feather, but most people can't hold me for more than a minute. What am I?

What can be fed, but dies if you give it water?

The answer to the first riddle is *a pillow*. The answer to the second riddle is *your breath*. The answer to the third riddle is *a fire*.

1. Most likely, an archaeologist would be interested in
   - **a.** what you ate for lunch today.
   - **b.** what you will eat for lunch tomorrow.
   - **c.** what people ate for lunch 1,000 years ago.
   - **d.** what people will eat for lunch in 1,000 years.
2. If you *etched* your name onto a stone, you
   - **a.** painted your name on the stone.
   - **b.** used a pencil to put your name on the stone.
   - **c.** pasted your name on the stone.
   - **d.** cut or carved your name into the stone.
3. Most likely, people from long ago
   - **a.** did not like riddles.
   - **b.** used riddles to teach and to have fun.
   - **c.** did not want people to know they told riddles.
   - **d.** thought riddles were not important.
4. Most likely, what is the answer to this riddle: *What goes up but never comes down?*
   - **a.** your age **b.** a balloon **c.** a kite **d.** an umbrella

Name: ______________________________

Puns

A *pun* is a kind of joke. It is a play on words. A pun uses words that sound similar but have different meanings. Some puns can come in the form of questions. For example, "Why are teddy bears never hungry? *They are always stuffed!*" "Why did the lion spit out the clown? *He tasted funny!*" "What do you call a sleeping bull? *You call it a bulldozer!*"

Some puns come in the form of statements. For example, "A boiled egg every morning is hard to beat." "Always trust a glue salesperson because they stick to their word." "A bicycle can't stand on its own because it is two-tired."

If you were just learning English, these puns would be very hard to understand. Think of all the different words you would have to know to understand these puns. You would have to know what a bull is. You would have to know that when you "doze off," you are sleeping. You would have to know that a bulldozer is a machine that pushes dirt. You would have to know that tired means you are sleepy and that bikes have tires.

1. To understand the pun about the teddy bear, what do you have to know?
   - **a.** Teddy bears are stuffed with a filling.
   - **b.** Teddy bears cannot be stuffed with food.
   - **c.** When you are stuffed, you are too full to eat anymore.
   - **d.** all of the above

2. A *pun* is a joke that
   - **a.** is a play on words.
   - **b.** always comes in the form of a question.
   - **c.** always comes in the form of a statement.
   - **d.** always is about words that share the same meaning.

3. Which of the following is an example of a pun?
   - **a.** What do baseball players hit with? *Bats!*
   - **b.** What do baseball players catch balls with? *Mitts!*
   - **c.** What do baseball players wear? *Baseball hats!*
   - **d.** What do baseball players eat on? *Home plates!*

4. Why did the author include examples of puns in this story?
   - **a.** to make the reader think about eggs
   - **b.** to see if the reader likes clowns
   - **c.** to help the reader understand what a pun is
   - **d.** to show how important questions are

5. What do you have to know about glue in order for the pun to be funny?
   - **a.** that you should not eat it
   - **b.** that it is sticky
   - **c.** that it smells
   - **d.** that it only works when it is warm

Name: ___________________________________

Ruby's Exact Weight

Opal said, "I will write your exact weight down on a piece of paper. If I get it wrong, I will do your chores tonight. If I get it right, you have to do my chores."

Ruby thought about it. Tonight was her night for clearing the table and taking out the garbage. It would be nice if Opal had to do those two tasks. Ruby then looked around. She didn't see a scale anywhere. She didn't think it possible that Opal could know how much she weighed. "Agreed," Ruby said. "You have to write down my exact weight on this piece of paper. If you don't write down my exact weight, you have to do my chores. You can't even be one pound off!"

Opal agreed. She wrote something down on the paper. When Ruby read what was on the paper, she started to laugh. "Very clever," she said. What had Opal written? She had written the words, *your exact weight*.

1. A *synonym* is a word that means the same thing as another word. What word is **not** a synonym for *chore*?
   a. task **b.** job **c.** game **d.** work
2. How do you know Ruby wasn't angry that she had to wash the dishes for Opal?
   a. She agreed.
   b. She looked around.
   c. She laughed.
   d. She wrote it down.
3. Most likely, Ruby thought that Opal
   a. was going to write her weight on a piece of paper.
   b. would know exactly what she weighed.
   c. would not need a scale to know how much she weighed.
   d. did not have any chores that night.
4. From the story, you can tell that a *scale* is
   a. used to write things.
   b. used to weigh things.
   c. used to play tricks.
   d. used to put garbage in.
5. This story is mainly about
   a. what chores Ruby had to do.
   b. a trick Ruby pulled on Opal.
   c. what chores Opal had to do.
   d. a trick Opal pulled on Ruby.

Name: ______________________________

Write On!

Pick one riddle, pun, or trick from the stories you read in this unit. Think about why someone who is just learning English might not understand this riddle, pun, or trick. Then, explain what the words mean in the riddle or pun, why the riddle or pun is funny, or why the trick worked.

When you are done, go back and reread what you wrote. Write down two of your sentences that have the letter *e* in them. Try to rewrite the two sentences without using an *e*. It will be very hard!

Name: ______________________________

Coughing Frogs

You catch a frog. While holding it in your hand, you witness something so strange that you wonder if you are dreaming. Is it really happening? Little frogs are jumping out of the big frog's mouth!

You know that frogs lay eggs. Little tadpoles hatch out of the eggs. The tadpoles grow bigger. They grow legs and turn into frogs. How is it possible that fully formed frogs are coming out of a big frog's mouth?

The frog is a Darwin frog. A male Darwin frog swallows the tadpoles as soon as they hatch. He keeps them in his vocal sac. They stay in his vocal sac for about 60 days. They grow in the sac and stay safe. When they are fully formed, the male frog coughs them out.

1. When you *witness* something, you
   - a. cough it out.
   - b. swallow it.
   - c. keep it safe.
   - d. see it.
2. About how long do the tadpoles stay in the vocal sac?
   - a. 6 days
   - b. 60 days
   - c. 6 weeks
   - d. 60 weeks
3. This story is mainly about
   - a. frogs.
   - b. coughing.
   - c. the Darwin frog.
   - d. tadpoles.
4. Why would you wonder if you were dreaming?
   - a. What you saw seemed too strange to be true.
   - b. You caught the frog when you were very sleepy.
   - c. You woke up the frog when you picked it up.
   - d. Nothing strange happens in dreams.

Name: ______________________

The Frog Prince

Splash! Harold jumped away as quickly as he could. He felt the cool water wash over his skin as he sunk below the surface. Harold floated on the water before scrambling up onto a log. "I'm safe out here," he thought with relief.

Turtle said, "Why are you out here on this log far away from shore? You need to let yourself get caught. That girl is a princess. If she kisses you, you will turn into a prince!"

"That's why I had to escape," Harold said. "I was a prince before, and I hated it! I had to wear a crown. I had to eat fruits and vegetables. I wasn't allowed to eat flies or mosquitoes! It was horrible!"

1. Where is the log?
   - a. close to shore in the water
   - b. far away from shore in the water
   - c. close to shore on the ground
   - d. far away from shore on the ground

2. Why didn't Harold like being a prince?
   - a. He had to eat fruits and vegetables.
   - b. He had to eat flies.
   - c. He had to eat mosquitoes.
   - d. He had to eat insects.

3. If you *get away*, you
   - a. escape.
   - b. float.
   - c. scramble.
   - d. sink.

4. What can you tell about Turtle from the story?
   - a. He was once a prince.
   - b. He does not want to be kissed.
   - c. He hopes he can have Harold's fruit.
   - d. He thinks Harold would like to be a prince.

Name: ______________________________

Ribbit, Ribbit

The pond was alive with sound. *Ribbit, ribbit, ribbit*, one kind of frog chorused. *Croak, croak, croak*, another kind of frog sang. The smallest frogs quietly hummed, *Chirrup, chirrup, chirrup*. The big bull frogs bellowed with a deep, *Buuullll, buuullll, buuullll*.

People came and built houses around the pond. The frogs stayed hidden in the water and mud where they were safe. Only their calls could be heard. *Ribbit, ribbit, ribbit*. *Croak, croak, croak*. *Chirrup, chirrup, chirrup*. *Buuullll, buuullll, buuullll*. Their voices filled the night air.

"Too loud!" the people cried. "We can't sleep! We must get rid of all those noisy frogs!" The people got rid of all the frogs. Night came. There were no more ribbits or croaks. There were no more chirrups or buuullls. Did the people enjoy the quiet? No, because there was a new sound. There was the *buzz, buzz, buzz* of thousands and thousands of mosquitoes.

1. From the story, you can tell that
   - **a.** the only safe place for frogs is in the mud.
   - **b.** there are more big frogs than little frogs.
   - **c.** different kinds of frogs have different sounds.
   - **d.** no one likes the sounds of frogs.
2. What happened first?
   - **a.** People enjoyed the quiet.
   - **b.** People got rid of the frogs.
   - **c.** People could hear mosquitoes buzzing.
   - **d.** People built houses around the pond.
3. Most likely, the author wanted you to learn what from the story?
   - **a.** Think about what might happen before you do it.
   - **b.** Make yourself feel better as soon as you can.
   - **c.** Don't worry about what is going to happen after you do something.
   - **d.** Frogs do nothing but make noise.
4. What did the smallest frogs do?
   - **a.** They bellowed. **b.** They hummed. **c.** They sang. **d.** They chorused.

Name: ______________________________

Winter Surprise

When people from Europe first came to North America, they got a surprise. They camped in the frozen snow. To stay warm, they lit a fire. Suddenly, they got a big surprise. They saw a frog hopping! They did not know where the frog came from or why it wasn't frozen.

The frog was a wood frog. Wood frogs have a special way of surviving when it is cold. When temperatures fall, the frog's body begins to shut down. It stops breathing. Its heartbeat decreases. Its muscles stop moving. The water in the frog's cells freezes, and the cells are filled with glucose and urea. The glucose and urea keep the cells from collapsing. The frog remains frozen until the temperature goes up. As the frog thaws, it starts breathing. Its heartbeat goes up. Its muscles start moving.

The men must have made the fire close to a frozen wood frog. The warmth from the fire thawed the frog. The men were surprised, but so was the frog! The frog did not expect to be hopping in snow!

1. This story is mainly about
   - **a.** frogs.
   - **b.** people from Europe.
   - **c.** a frog that can survive freezing temperatures.
   - **d.** where people made a fire.

2. When something *thaws*, it
   - **a.** freezes.
   - **b.** warms up.
   - **c.** shuts down.
   - **d.** collapses.

3. A wood frog's cells are filled with
   - **a.** glucose and water.
   - **b.** water and urea.
   - **c.** glucose and ice.
   - **d.** urea and glucose.

4. One reason a wood frog may need to freeze in the winter is because
   - **a.** not enough people light fires in the snow.
   - **b.** snow is white.
   - **c.** it can't hop as far when the wind is blowing.
   - **d.** it has a difficult time finding food.

5. What must happen before the wood frog's heartbeat decreases?
   - **a.** The temperature must go up.
   - **b.** The temperature must go down.
   - **c.** The snow must melt.
   - **d.** The frog must start to hop.

Name: ______________________________

Surprise Pet

Tom wanted a pet so much that it hurt. First, he asked for a cat, but his parents told him a cat was too big. "We live in a tiny apartment in the city," they said. "A pet is not a good idea unless it is small and easy to care for."

Tom was sad, but one day, his father surprised him with a tadpole. "When it changes into a frog, you can keep it in this small glass cage," Tom's father said.

Tom was very happy. He took good care of his tadpole. He fed it daily and made sure its water was clean. Every day he looked to see how much it had grown. When it started to grow legs, he was very happy. When the tadpole became a frog, Tom thought it would stop growing. It didn't!

It grew as big as a house cat! It jumped ten feet in a single hop! That's when Tom found out he had a Goliath frog. The Goliath frog is the biggest frog in the world.

1. If there were one more paragraph to the story, what would most likely happen?

- **a.** Tom would give his frog to the zoo.
- **b.** Tom's dad would give him a house cat.
- **c.** Tom would keep his frog in the small glass cage.
- **d.** Tom would get another Goliath frog.

2. How do you know Tom's father didn't know that the tadpole he brought home was from a Goliath frog?

- **a.** He said a pet is not a good idea.
- **b.** He said pets should be easy to care for.
- **c.** He said they lived in a tiny apartment.
- **d.** He said a pet cat was too big.

3. An *antonym* is a word that means the opposite of another word. What word is an antonym for *goliath*?

a. huge **b.** tiny **c.** giant **d.** large

4. Most likely, how did Tom's parents feel when the frog kept growing?

a. happy **b.** merry **c.** uneasy **d.** joyful

5. How far could Tom's frog jump?

a. 1 foot **b.** 8 feet **c.** 10 feet **d.** 18 feet

Name: ______________________________

Write On!

For each of the frogs you learned about in Unit 16, explain how its unique behavior or size allows it to survive in its natural environment.

Darwin frog

____

____

____

____

____

wood frog

____

____

____

____

____

Goliath frog

____

____

____

____

____

Name: ______________________________

The Nut That Isn't

Its name says it is. It isn't. The peanut is not a nut. Peanuts are legumes. Like peas, peanuts are edible seeds inside pods. They grow under the ground. They do not grow on trees like walnuts or almonds.

Many people think that peanut butter was a brilliant invention. It tastes good. It has lots of protein. Who made it first? Early peanut plants were native to South America. Researchers believe the first peanut butter was made hundreds of years ago. The ancient Incans and Aztecs made it. They were the first to eat ground-up peanuts.

Lots of peanut butter is sold today. It comes in jars. Think of a 12-ounce jar. How many peanuts are in that one jar? There are about 500!

1. You can tell from the story that *ground* has more than one meaning. It can mean
   - **a.** mashed up *or* under.
   - **b.** dirt *or* in a jar.
   - **c.** mashed up *or* in a jar.
   - **d.** dirt *or* mashed up.

2. Why isn't a peanut a nut?
   - **a.** It grows on a tree.
   - **b.** It is a legume.
   - **c.** It is like a walnut.
   - **d.** It is edible.

3. Why do some people think peanut butter was a brilliant invention?
   - **a.** It tastes good and is filled with protein.
   - **b.** It was made by the ancient Incans and Aztecs.
   - **c.** It grows inside a pod.
   - **d.** It was first made hundreds of years ago.

4. About how many peanuts are there in a 12-ounce jar of peanut butter?
   - **a.** about 5
   - **b.** about 50
   - **c.** about 500
   - **d.** about 5,000

Name: ______________________________

Nut Party

Mr. Presley's class was having a nut party. Every student was bringing nuts. The nuts would be put in a bowl, mixed together, and shared. Everyone would get to taste a variety of nuts.

Mia brought walnuts. She brought a whole bag. Logan brought cashews. He brought a whole can. Sarita brought almonds. She brought a big jar. Nate brought pistachios. He brought a whole bag. Taylor didn't bring walnuts, cashews, almonds, or pistachios. She didn't bring a bag, a can, or a jar. She only brought one nut.

Taylor only brought one nut, but this nut weighed more than everyone else's nuts combined! Taylor brought a *coco-de-mer palm nut*. This huge seed is the biggest nut in the world. It can weigh 40 pounds!

1. Who brought the pistachios?
   a. Nate **b.** Mia **c.** Logan **d.** Sarita
2. If there is a *variety* of something,
   a. every kind is big.
   b. every kind is small.
   c. there is only one kind.
   d. there is more than one kind.
3. Most likely, how did Mr. Presley look when he saw what Taylor brought?
   a. angry **b.** disappointed **c.** surprised **d.** sad
4. Most likely, what lesson led to the class having a nut party?
   a. studying the difference between a seed and a nut
   b. locating where the Nile River is
   c. discussing the difference between a pond and a lake
   d. locating where the biggest tree lives

Name: ____________________________________

More Than Seven

Jack's mother said, "Go to town. Sell the cow. Last time, you traded the cow for seven magic beans. The beans grew into a giant beanstalk. You climbed up the stalk and saw a huge house. When you went in, you saw a giant, and he almost ate you! You had to race down the stalk, get an axe, and chop it down before the giant could descend. That giant was almost the end of us! So this time, listen to me. Trade the cow for more than seven beans!"

Jack came back from town several hours later. Jack's mother asked where the money from the cow was. That was when Jack said, "You told me I had to trade the cow for more than seven beans." He opened his hand, and in the center of his palm there was what looked like a bit of dust. "Orchid seeds!" Jack said happily. "They are the world's smallest seeds, and I traded our one cow for one thousand of them!"

1. "More Than Seven" is a fiction story, but there is a fact in it. Which of the following is a fact?
   - **a.** There are magic beans.
   - **b.** Jack climbed a giant beanstalk.
   - **c.** Orchid seeds are the world's smallest seeds.
   - **d.** A giant almost ate Jack.
2. Where would you most likely find this story?
   - **a.** in a science book
   - **b.** in a book about seeds and plants
   - **c.** in a children's book of fairy tales
   - **d.** in a book about selling and buying
3. When the giant was *descending*, he was
   a. going down. **b.** going up. **c.** staying still. **d.** getting bigger.
4. How do you know Jack's mother might not be so happy with his one thousand orchid seeds?
   - **a.** She asked to see the seeds.
   - **b.** She asked where the money from the cow was.
   - **c.** She asked what the bit of dust was in his palm.
   - **d.** She asked where Jack was going to plant the seeds.

Name: ____________________

An Invention from Seeds

How do plants disperse their seeds? Some seeds are inside of fruits. Animals eat the fruit. They digest the fruit, but the seed comes out in the animals' droppings. There is a bat in South America. It is called the *short-tailed fruit bat*. This bat can scatter up to 60,000 seeds in just one night!

Other plants have seeds coated with tiny hooks. Animals brush against the plant, and the seeds get caught in their fur. The animal disperses the seeds by carrying them away!

In 1948, a man named George de Mestral and his dog went hiking. They both came home with burrs stuck to them. Mestral looked at the sticky seeds by using a microscope. He saw that the burrs had tiny hooks. Then, Mestral started thinking. He worked for eight years. When he was done, he had invented something. He had invented Velcro. Velcro has two strips. One strip has thousands of tiny hooks. The other strip has thousands of tiny loops. The strips stick to each other. They are easy to pull apart.

1. When something is *dispersed,* it is

a. digested. **b.** sticky. **c.** spread around. **d.** easy to pull apart.

2. From the first paragraph, you can tell that

a. some plants and animals need each other.
b. plants do not want their fruits to be eaten.
c. bats only eat insects.
d. all seeds are easily digested.

3. How long did Mestral work on his invention?

a. seven months **b.** eight months **c.** seven years **d.** eight years

4. This story is mainly about

a. one way of dispersing seeds and one invention.
b. two ways of dispersing seeds and one invention.
c. one way of dispersing seeds and two inventions.
d. two ways of dispersing seeds and two inventions.

5. By reading this story, what can a person learn about inventions?

a. Inventions always have two parts.
b. Most inventions have thousands of parts.
c. All inventions are made quickly.
d. Ideas for inventions may come from daily life.

Name: ______________________________

Not Me First!

Mrs. Carver's class was having a lesson on the cashew. Mrs. Carver said, "The tree is native to Brazil. Today, cashews are not just grown in South America. They are grown in Asia and Africa, too.

"The seed is surrounded by a double shell. The shell contains a poison. Touch it, and your skin will burn. Long ago, people learned to roast the cashews. Roasting the cashews got rid of the poison. They learned to roast the cashews outside. This is because the smoke from the burning cashews was toxic. The poison in the smoke could damage their lungs. If they roasted the cashews outside, it was easier to avoid the smoke."

Yazmin raised her hand. She said, "You have told us what goes into processing this nut. It sounds like a lot of work. It makes me think about long ago. It makes me wonder. I would not have wanted to be the first person to eat a cashew. I would have been afraid of being poisoned. Who was the first person to find out the nut was edible? Who said, 'Me first!'?"

1. From the story, you can tell that

- **a.** most foods do not need to be processed.
- **b.** for some foods, a lot of processing is needed.
- **c.** processed foods taste the best.
- **d.** foods are processed so they will become toxic.

2. When something is *edible*,

- **a.** it is toxic.
- **b.** it is poison.
- **c.** it can be safely eaten.
- **d.** it has been roasted.

3. This story is mainly about

- **a.** nuts.
- **b.** cashew nuts.
- **c.** processing different kinds of nuts.
- **d.** people from long ago.

4. Long ago, how might people have learned that the cashew nut was safe to eat?

- **a.** They cracked it with their bare hands.
- **b.** They didn't care about their health.
- **c.** They had too much food.
- **d.** They saw animals safely eating the nuts.

5. You are not told whether the cashew tree grows in

- **a.** Europe.
- **b.** Asia.
- **c.** Africa.
- **d.** South America.

Name: ______________________________

Write On!

In Unit 17, you learned about several different types of seeds. These seeds have different strategies for survival and *dispersal*. Create your own "perfect" seed. Make sure to describe how the seed looks, how it protects itself, and how it is dispersed to new areas. Next, compare and contrast your seed to one of the seeds in Unit 17. Explain why you think your seed has a better chance of surviving in nature.

Tracking Sheet

Unit 1 *(pages 6–11)*		Unit 7 *(pages 42–47)*		Unit 13 *(pages 78–83)*	
Snorkeling		Tied Together		Only Twelve	
The Periscope		The Fastest Runner		Why She Wept	
A Fable About Wishing		Live from the Racetrack!		A Piece of Space	
Something Scary		An Extra Leg		Dinosaurs and Erosion	
Some Kind of Giant		Shark Attack		Missing!	
Write On!		Write On!		Write On!	
Unit 2 *(pages 12–17)*		**Unit 8** *(pages 48–53)*		**Unit 14** *(pages 84–89)*	
A Great Gymnast		Sky Fish		What Am I?	
Fast, Faster, Fastest		The Wager		The Best Job	
Sonic Boom		Hurricane at Sea		Fact or Fiction?	
Closing the Gap		Storm Danger		Planning Ahead	
Charlie and Dill		Alex and Bonnie		A San Story	
Write On!		Write On!		Write On!	
Unit 3 *(pages 18–23)*		**Unit 9** *(pages 54–59)*		**Unit 15** *(pages 90–95)*	
Hero Dogs		One of Seven		What Did You Say?	
Moose Alley		Impossible House		Something's Missing	
Dangerous Ice		Six or Seven?		Riddles	
Stove Sitting		Longest and Largest		Puns	
What Word?		The Liar		Ruby's Exact Weight	
Write On!		Write On!		Write On!	
Unit 4 *(pages 24–29)*		**Unit 10** *(pages 60–65)*		**Unit 16** *(pages 96–101)*	
A Rule for Walls		Not for Sale		Coughing Frogs	
What Glowed in the Dark?		The New Word		The Frog Prince	
A Long Sleep		Cinquain Poems		Ribbit, Ribbit	
When the Sun Sets		Disaster		Winter Surprise	
The Missing Hotel		When April Comes		Surprise Pet	
Write On!		Write On!		Write On!	
Unit 5 *(pages 30–35)*		**Unit 11** *(pages 66–71)*		**Unit 17** *(pages 102–107)*	
Joey for Dinner?		The Tree Octopus		The Nut That Isn't	
The Strange Pouch		Seeing Through Walls		Nut Party	
Hero Kangaroo		Eye Test		More Than Seven	
Unlikely Friends		The TMW		An Invention from Seeds	
Surprise Answers		Fake News		Not Me First!	
Write On!		Write On!		Write On!	
Unit 6 *(pages 36–41)*		**Unit 12** *(pages 72–77)*			
The Open Window		Fortune Cookies			
All Wrong		Dana's Invention			
Riddle Play		100 Years Diary			
Bee Thrashing		Buttons			
Only Green		Ali's Invention			
Write On!		Write On!			

Answer Key

Answer Key

Unit 1

Snorkeling (page 6)

1. c 2. a 3. d 4. b

The Periscope (page 7)

1. c 2. d 3. a 4. d

A Fable About Wishing (page 8)

1. d 2. c 3. b 4. b

Something Scary (page 9)

1. a 2. c 3. b 4. c 5. b

Some Kind of Giant (page 10)

1. a 2. b 3. d 4. a 5. c

Unit 2

A Great Gymnast (page 12)

1. c 2. d 3. b 4. a

Fast, Faster, Fastest (page 13)

1. d 2. b 3. c 4. b

Sonic Boom (page 14)

1. d 2. b 3. a 4. c

Closing the Gap (page 15)

1. a 2. a 3. d 4. b 5. d

Charlie and Dill (page 16)

1. b 2. c 3. a 4. d 5. c

Unit 3

Hero Dogs (page 18)

1. b 2. c 3. a 4. b

Moose Alley (page 19)

1. d 2. c 3. a 4. d

Dangerous Ice (page 20)

1. a 2. b 3. c 4. d

Stove Sitting (page 21)

1. d 2. a 3. c 4. b 5. d

What Word? (page 22)

1. c 2. d 3. b 4. a 5. a

Unit 4

A Rule for Walls (page 24)

1. b 2. c 3. b 4. d

What Glowed in the Dark? (page 25)

1. d 2. a 3. c 4. b

A Long Sleep (page 26)

1. d 2. b 3. a 4. c

When the Sun Sets (page 27)

1. a 2. b 3. d 4. d 5. a

The Missing Hotel (page 28)

1. c 2. d 3. a 4. a 5. c

Unit 5

Joey for Dinner? (page 30)

1. a 2. c 3. d 4. b

The Strange Pouch (page 31)

1. c 2. d 3. a 4. a

Hero Kangaroo (page 32)

1. d 2. a 3. b 4. b

Unlikely Friends (page 33)

1. c 2. d 3. a 4. c 5. b

Surprise Answers (page 34)

1. b 2. b 3. c 4. d 5. a

Unit 6

The Open Window (page 36)

1. c 2. c 3. a 4. b

All Wrong (page 37)

1. b 2. a 3. d 4. b

Riddle Play (page 38)

1. d 2. a 3. c 4. c

Bee Thrashing (page 39)

1. a 2. b 3. d 4. b 5. c

Only Green (page 40)

1. d 2. c 3. a 4. d 5. b

Answer Key *(cont.)*

Unit 7

Tied Together (page 42)

1. d 2. b 3. d 4. c

The Fastest Runner (page 43)

1. c 2. b 3. a 4. d

Live from the Racetrack! (page 44)

1. d 2. c 3. b 4. b

An Extra Leg (page 45)

1. b 2. d 3. c 4. a 5. d

Shark Attack (page 46)

1. a 2. a 3. c 4. d 5. c

Unit 8

Sky Fish (page 48)

1. c 2. a 3. c 4. a

The Wager (page 49)

1. a 2. c 3. d 4. b

Hurricane at Sea (page 50)

1. a 2. b 3. a 4. c

Storm Danger (page 51)

1. b 2. d 3. b 4. d 5. c

Alex and Bonnie (page 52)

1. d 2. d 3. c 4. c 5. b

Unit 9

One of Seven (page 54)

1. d 2. a 3. c 4. d

Impossible House (page 55)

1. b 2. b 3. a 4. c

Six or Seven? (page 56)

1. c 2. d 3. a 4. a

Longest and Largest (page 57)

1. a 2. a 3. d 4. b 5. d

The Liar (page 58)

1. d 2. c 3. b 4. a 5. c

Unit 10

Not for Sale (page 60)

1. d 2. a 3. b 4. b

The New Word (page 61)

1. c 2. b 3. a 4. d

Cinquain Poems (page 62)

1. b 2. c 3. d 4. a

Disaster (page 63)

1. a 2. d 3. c 4. c 5. b

When April Comes (page 64)

1. c 2. b 3. d 4. a 5. c

Unit 11

The Tree Octopus (page 66)

1. a 2. c 3. d 4. c

Seeing Through Walls (page 67)

1. b 2. b 3. c 4. c

Eye Test (page 68)

1. d 2. a 3. c 4. d

The TMW (page 69)

1. c 2. d 3. b 4. a 5. a

Fake News (page 70)

1. d 2. b 3. b 4. b 5. a

Unit 12

Fortune Cookies (page 72)

1. b 2. d 3. b 4. d

Dana's Invention (page 73)

1. c 2. b 3. d 4. a

100 Years Diary (page 74)

1. b 2. d 3. a 4. c

Buttons (page 75)

1. d 2. c 3. a 4. b 5. c

Ali's Invention (page 76)

1. a 2. a 3. c 4. d 5. b

Answer Key *(cont.)*

Unit 13

Only Twelve (page 78)

1. b 2. b 3. c 4. a

Why She Wept (page 79)

1. c 2. a 3. d 4. a

A Piece of Space (page 80)

1. d 2. c 3. c 4. b

Dinosaurs and Erosion (page 81)

1. c 2. d 3. a 4. d 5. b

Missing! (page 82)

1. d 2. c 3. a 4. b 5. d

Unit 14

What Am I? (page 84)

1. c 2. c 3. b 4. a

The Best Job (page 85)

1. d 2. a 3. b 4. c

Fact or Fiction? (page 86)

1. c 2. a 3. a 4. c

Planning Ahead (page 87)

1. a 2. b 3. d 4. b 5. a

A San Story (page 88)

1. b 2. d 3. a 4. d 5. c

Unit 15

What Did You Say? (page 90)

1. c 2. b 3. c 4. c

Something's Missing (page 91)

1. b 2. d 3. b 4. a

Riddles (page 92)

1. c 2. d 3. b 4. a

Puns (page 93)

1. d 2. a 3. d 4. c 5. b

Ruby's Exact Weight (page 94)

1. c 2. c 3. a 4. b 5. d

Unit 16

Coughing Frogs (page 96)

1. d 2. b 3. c 4. a

The Frog Prince (page 97)

1. b 2. a 3. a 4. d

Ribbit, Ribbit (page 98)

1. c 2. d 3. a 4. b

Winter Surprise (page 99)

1. c 2. b 3. d 4. d 5. b

Surprise Pet (page 100)

1. a 2. d 3. b 4. c 5. c

Unit 17

The Nut That Isn't (page 102)

1. d 2. b 3. a 4. c

Nut Party (page 103)

1. a 2. d 3. c 4. a

More Than Seven (page 104)

1. c 2. c 3. a 4. b

An Invention from Seeds (page 105)

1. c 2. a 3. d 4. b 5. d

Not Me First! (page 106)

1. b 2. c 3. b 4. d 5. a